Making a Difference

A Slice of Life for a Dog Behaviourist

by

Christine Emerson

D1390049

Table of Contents

Max

Clint

Never dismiss the obvious

Something not smelling quite right

Striking a pose with Madonna

Finding Fern

Fern and the Jack Russell

Haunted Happenings

Don't make me go out......

Poppy

The privilege of meeting some people

Goldie and the mouse

Ben and the handbag

Puppies need peace too

Swap! Dog for a second-hand TV

Trixie

Hidden suburban danger

A 'thank you' letter

Basil & Sally

Marley

Westie – anxious to get home

Frank

Buster

Chudley

Do little dogs need training?

Henry

Sasha

Bullseye

Tommy

To the moon and back, with Bracken

Getting cosy with Butch

Although the stories in this book are true, the names of pets and people have been changed to protect their identity.

Copyright © Christine Emerson 2014

All rights reserved

No part of this publication may be reproduced, stored in a retrieval system, or tranmitted, in any form, or by any means, without the prior permission in writing of the author, nor be otherwise circulated in any form of binding or cover other than that in which it is published.

For Sam

I am so sorry. I wish I'd known then what I know now. But because of you, because we met, many dogs have been and will be, better understood

Many years ago, in the early 1980s, before I knew anything about dog behaviour, my dog Sam showed a lot of aggression towards me. He had nipped and growled before but we had stopped that with a quick smack, a tap on the nose, hands on our hips and a sharp word.

My vet and my trainer told me his show of aggression was because he was trying to be 'top dog' and that I should be more "dominant", show him who's boss by using more overpowering aggression. The shows of aggression, admittedly, had increased over the years, but my vet and trainer told me that was because I wasn't being tough enough.

One day, I was in the garden with Sam, who was by then 7 years old. I was late for work but he was refusing to come back in the house and so I approached him and raised my hand to grab his collar. This time, he launched at me in a frenzy of snarling teeth and bit me deeply several times from my head to the back of my calves. He had had enough! After an overnight stay in hospital getting cleaned up, I returned home tearful to the prospect of having to put my friend to sleep.

Sam was a brown dog, medium sized, a cross-breed of many generations. My husband and I had adopted him from a local dog pound, operated by Drove Vets in Wiltshire. (Little did I know that, a couple of decades later, I would be the Head of a Behaviour Services department for that same vets). When we adopted him at 7 months of age, we didn't have a clue about looking after a dog and relied totally on the advice at our local training classes and our vet in the next town. Like so many dog owners, we didnt realise how little vets and dog trainers knew about dog behaviour back then.

Desperate to find an alternative to the euthanasia, I asked around and made many telephone calls to find a canine expert who successfully trained dogs without using aggression of any sort. I came across the most wonderful lady

– Gwen Bailey. She told me to "stop frightening my dog". It was music to my ears. It had never occurred to me that Sam might be scared of my hands – he never knew when they were going to stroke his ears or grab his collar! I asked "Why has the fear come to a head at 7 years old?". Her reply was simple,"With age comes maturity and social confidence. He now has the confidence to express how he may have been feeling for many years".

Within two weeks of me trying a new approach Sam had stopped showing any sign of aggression. Over the following few months I learned just from self-education, that Sam's growling only meant "please stop doing that, if you continue I may have to bite you" and that we only smack for as long as we can get away with it (could that be applied to smacking children? That's probably another book).

As I learned more and applied confidence-building, kind and respectful rules and boundaries, I saw Sam become a loving and trusting dog. Yes, there was the odd occasion when I would see him stiffen and one time he grasped my hand with his mouth, but I softened my posture, whispered "Sam, No", waited for his response and whispered praise when he backed off. He died a happy dog at the age of eighteen.

This experience had such a profound effect on both Sam and myself that I decided to learn as much as I could and come up with an alternative way of training. There were no qualifications available at the time, nor associations that you could be proud to be a member of, but I was determined to help other dog owners in the way that Gwen Bailey helped me.

For the first 15 years I was self-employed. My best friend had persuaded me to offer advice to the public and charge! She said, "If you can be helped in such a profound way by just a telephone call, perhaps you can help others who want to find another way of training their dog."

I felt very guilty taking money from people when I had little proof that my methods would help *them*. I was going to spend two hours in someone's home, finding the true cause by sheer logic and finding the true emotional state of the dog. I read everything. If it seemed logical it was probably worth remembering. I learned about medical causes for unwanted dog behaviour and decided to be cheeky and visit as many training classes as I could, in the hope I would find someone else with a kindred approach. It was then that I came across the APDT (Association of Pet Dog Trainers) and stopped feeling alone.

The APDT are a wonderful organisation whose members are expected to use kind and respectful methods of training and they will assess you to a high standard before offering membership. I met some terrifically knowledgeable Behaviourists in the APDT and so was tickled pink to be granted membership as one. A member needs to prove that they have continued to learn and stay ahead with research and the latest understanding in dog behaviour but they'll also advise where to get that education. There were no degree courses in animal behaviour in those days but I gained distinctions in every other level of qualification available in the specialty of dog behaviour. I was so relieved – with grades this good I must have been practicing correctly and giving out the right advice. I was on a roll.

From a spare room I slowly gathered essential equipment, shopping around for alternatives to things like choke chains. I was not well off and so chose to beg for donations of equipment, toys, food-dispensers etc. then came across Mary, of Champion Pet Supplies in Nuneaton. Mary trusted that I would give a shop catalogue to every client if she gave me a free box of goodies. This lady didn't know me and simply chose to trust I was good to my word; I think some of my early clients still buy from her, via mail-order, today.

I literally walked into every vet, pet shop and boarding kennel in Wiltshire, introducing myself and this new-fandangled service of Behaviour Counselling. Instead of sending a barking dog to training classes to get it solved, I was going to spend time seeing the behaviour where it happened and spend time over the detail so it doesn't come back. It was a hit!

Vets at that time didn't have a clue how to solve behaviour issues and were chuffed to be able to pass the owners on to someone else. I will never forget the welcome I had at Drove Vets. They always were and still are, the most forward-thinking veterinary surgery I have ever come across.

In contrast, I remember one day going in to a small veterinary practice in Swindon, asking if I could have 10 minutes of the veterinary surgeon's time. The timid receptionist went behind the scenes to put the proposal to the veterinary surgeon owner of the practice. A scowling hulk of a man appeared at the door, intimated I should come with him, sat down with a great 'humph', crossed his arms and spat "Okay, impress me." As you can imagine, I didn't. That man was determined never to be impressed by life, and everything in it. He had one of those miserable faces that it takes a lifetime to achieve and he was a fool, because a few years later he was to need me.

Max

As my confidence grew with success and satisfied clients, so did my foolishness. I thought my talent would keep me safe and worked with many a confident dog showing aggression, without them being muzzled.

One day, I learned my lesson. Max, the German Shepherd, was known to show aggression to people on walks, so to assess his behaviour, I set myself up as a passing stranger in the local park. All I had was reassurance from the young owners that the dog had only lunged and never injured, as well as the assurance from the lady holding his long lead that she wouldn't let go.

I walked past her and the dog, in the opposite direction, 50 feet apart and the dog's gaze never left me. He lowered his head, jutted his jaw and aligned his spine, readying to shoot at me like an arrow. Totally ignoring the dog, I passed and, when 300 yards away, I slowly turned to see if his intent had diminished but instead saw 40 kilograms of dog readying to tear straight for me.

He took off, gathered speed and reached the end of his lead with such strength that the lead was snapped straight out of the owner's hand and was whipping along the grass behind him. I bellowed "GET THAT LEAD!" but that lady was having trouble catching up. She looked absolutely terrified. I froze, hunched my shoulders and avoided eye contact. The silent animal launched himself through the air with teeth bared and got hold of the arm of my coat with his teeth. At the exact second he made contact with me, his owner threw herself at the trailing lead, as if she was saving the dog from the enormities of his actions. He ripped my coat sleeve, leaving it flapping limply, but thanks to the owner grasping the lead at the last minute, I had absolutely no injury.

What a fool! What a lesson! I learned never to trust an owner's judgement and to expect every dog I visited, and their house-mates, to be hostile. I had nightmares about being attacked by German Shepherds for many months, and doubted my choice of a career. Thanks to a very supportive husband and great friends, I continued the journey, only to find myself in Salisbury meeting Clint.

Clint

Clint was a Great Dane, who was fed up to the teeth with being touched by strangers when he walked down the High Street.

We don't like to be touched by strangers and so it amazes me that there are so many humans about who expect dogs to put up with it. This 'young chap' initially backed off, but when his well-meaning owners encouraged him to meet the over-familiar stranger he snapped. He wasn't allowed to back off so he made the stranger back off.

So I thought that it was going to be a simple matter of explaining what was happening from Clint's point of view, and suggesting that he wear a jacket printed with 'Dog in Training'. These jackets are great for getting people to keep their hands to themselves.

But it had taken his owners many months to realise that help was needed and by the time I met Clint in his home for the initial chat, he was monumentally irritated by all strangers, whether in the High street or in his home. Unfortunately for me, his naive people were quite oblivious to the depth of Clint's simmering anger.

I settled in the cosy armchair and in walked Clint. Now all Great Danes walk relatively slowly, but this one was walking slowly with a very controlled pace; his eye contact with me was held a little longer than necessary. As he approached me, I noticed that his feet stretched upwards just an inch in height, you could almost hear the creak of flexing muscles, despite me making no move or indication that I would touch him (in fact, I folded my arms to show my lack of intention). His stiff tail rose in height like a flag-pole and he chose to stop only when his face was two inches away from mine – his chops were at face height. He stared me loudly in the eye, a silent message pretty similar to "take your bag girl, and leave".

I had learned by that time that noisy dogs, those putting on a display of threat, are not usually the biters; it's the silent ones with confident body language that can be. My instinct was to turn my face away from his just slightly but when I did that, Clint simultaneously moved his face back into mine. The owners were overjoyed to see this "He likes you!" they chimed. "I don't think he does" I replied quietly "I'll explain it to you once you are able to get him out of the room." This startled the owners, why would this 'expert' need to have our Clint out the room? "Are you frightened of him?" they smirked. "No" I replied a little irritated "I know my stuff and I know he wants one of us to leave the room. Can you make it him, please?"

They were virtually laughing at me but I was determined to be a little more clever this time. I had to stick to my instinct; that gut reaction that you must never ignore. They removed Clint and I instantly relaxed. Some dogs bring an electric atmosphere to a room.

We chatted. They liked the idea of the jacket, which I had created and sold, and I added the suggestion of a muzzle. I didn't want this to escalate into a bite, and the muzzle would also have the same effect of keeping people away. Two tools could mean seeing positive results twice as quickly, but no, they didn't want their Clint looking vicious, they wanted him to look friendly and.........dare I say it, approachable.

Some people, you simply can't help

Never dismiss the obvious

I received a call from a lady who needed help with her dog, who was constantly licking her bottom (not the lady's but its own).

Now I would never give a diagnosis and tips over the phone, as it is based on the owner's interpretation and of course, I don't make any money from giving free advice. If I'm not earning money I'm no longer in practice and the dogs suffer. However, I need to ascertain from the initial telephone call that it is a behaviour issue and not one for the vets.

I talked with the lady about the possibility of worms, blocked anal glands and boredom. The lady was a poor historian and answered all my questions monosyllabically. I concluded that she should visit the vets to have the dog's bottom looked at and she agreed to arrange this. Just as I was about to put the phone down the conversation took an interesting turn:

Owner: "she's got a sweet stuck to her bottom. "

Me: "pardon?"

Owner: "a sweet stuck to her bottom."

Me: "like a boiled sweet?"

Owner: "yes"

Me: "how long has she had that stuck to her bottom?"

Owner (to someone else): "how long has she had that sweet stuck to her bottom?"

Voice in the background: "about three weeks"

'No wonder she licks her bottom', I thought, she has the tastiest bottom in Wiltshire! She must have sat on an unwrapped boiled sweet and it was there to stay!

I advised the lady to make a vet appointment as soon as possible, put the phone down, put my head in my hands saying, "Give me strength!"

Something not smelling quite right

Have you ever met an Italian Spinone? If not, you must. They are big, blond, shaggy dogs with mad-looking moustaches that could match that of any Galloping Major.

My house-visits included two of these handsome creatures, aged 8 and 2 years, who lived very peacefully together. They were both entire (they had not had their testicles removed) and this, quite typically, had resulted in producing two very settled companions.

The younger one had started to cock his leg outside on walks at approximately 7 months of age, but only now, at 2 years of age, had he suddenly started to cock his leg and pee indoors.

Everything about their lifestyle and that of the owners, had been steady and consistent for the past year. There had been no change in diet, the home environment or relationships. They had had no canine visitors, the scent from which may encourage a resident dog to feel the need to cover up. What had changed?

When I looked around their home there were no fence panels down, the exposure from which sometimes makes dog feel reluctant to toilet in the garden. They didn't think a neighbour's cat had got in, nor did they know of any bitches in the neighbourhood that may be in season. What could it be?

I asked if I could take a break and whilst enjoying a strong cup of tea, I asked myself 'why would a dog suddenly want to make their home smell more of them than it currently does?' Something in the home is smelling differently and making the younger dog feel uncomfortable. No new sofas, they hadn't had the carpets cleaned.

Then it came to me! "Is the older dog acting differently in any way?" I asked "No, he's not" replied the lady owner "but male dogs seem to be picking on him lately." Bingo! That was it! The 8 year old dog is having a surge in testosterone and a common cause for a peak in testosterone at that age is extra tissue forming in his rear end, perhaps a tumour.

Testosterone levels rise at about 7-8 months, peak at 12-18 months, fall slightly but stay steady, and then after the age of 5-6 years steadily fall. So a sudden change in the behaviour of male dogs towards an older dog can mean they are smelling strongly of testosterone and other related chemicals in the body, and that's not good.

I'm a great believer in not neutering male dogs until they are about 4 years of age, unless they are showing unwanted testosterone-related behaviour but, as with girl dogs, this 8 year old Spinone should not have got to this age with his 'bits' as they can often turn cancerous.

Within a week the vet had confirmed the poor fella had prostate cancer, which was swiftly removed. It had not spread, however and he recovered well. No longer would the DVD player be covered in pee! They returned to being settled friends snuggling by the fire, of the house that smelled fresh once again.

Striking a pose with Madonna

Madonna helped one angry dog I met. This medium-sized cross-breed had been angry for years, lunging and growling at most visitors (but only visitors to his home, never when away in their caravan).

I was called out after he had bitten a visitor who then threatened to report the incident to the police. The bite happened in a 'private place'. The Dangerous Dogs Act currently only covers public areas or private areas where the dog has been invited; aggression to people say inside a home, is covered by a Civil Act. But I wasn't going to tell them that it's harder to prosecute for an act of aggression in a private place. I wanted them to take this as seriously as possible; this was one angry dog!

So there I was, sat cosily in an armchair whilst the muzzled dog threw me a hardened stare, threatening unimaginable damage if I didn't get out of his house, immediately!

I needed to find what sooths his soul, what makes him happy - how can we get his mood under a human's control? We addressed the cause of aggression and motivation for its continuance, but how are we going to get this dog in a positive frame of mind, so he can look forward to visitors coming?

As the conversation continued I asked the owners, a lovely young couple, what his favourite game was – and it didn't need to be a toy. They thought about it for approximately half a second, looked at each other with a giggle in their eyes and said, "Musical Statues, but only to Madonna's 'Vogue'." "Sorry, how does that work with a dog?" I asked. "Shall we show you?" they replied enthusiastically. I was delighted to sit back while they prepared for the game.

As soon as the track started to play, the dog completely forgot about me. The humans stood up and danced around the lounge and the dog joined in, swinging his head, wriggling around, he only had eyes for his owners. Then the music stopped and so did the dog! Nothing moved but his eyes. With obvious glee, the music started again and so did the dancing. It was a joy. During the remaining couple of minutes of the song, I moved around the room to see if it would provoke and distract the dog. But no, he was lost in Madonna's 'Vogue', striking a pose!

After much searching we found a doorbell contraption that would play any recording you made when the doorbell button was pressed. I asked them to make a list of his favourite things and we kept them away until a visitor arrived, therefore, visitors were associated with this dog's favourite tune on the doorbell and the good things that were timed with it.

We had to bribe even the bravest people to help us out. Anyone who could follow requests and not get too touchy-feely with him would turn up any time, day or night for a small party and just slip away again.

Ensuring the dog doesn't have a chance to be aggressive, a consistent response to better behaviour, management of visitors' behaviour and not rushing the process resulted in this dog, 6 months later, looking for visitors out his front window - not to take chunks out of them, but to get the party started!

Finding Fern

After Sam, I went looking for a well-bred black Labrador puppy. She was to be a pet, but if she enjoyed socialising (and some dogs, like some people, just don't like socialising) I would use her as a stooge dog.

Black dogs can be perceived as hostile by other dogs. A dog's vision is poor on contrast; that's why nature helps define the picture by giving black lip-liner, eye-liner, a flash of contrasting colour at the end of the tail, to emphasise tail height and even a contrasting colour to the hair around the bottom, and the actual bottom hole! Yet, when a totally black dog's face approaches, the other dog can't see the expression and assess whether it is friendly or not. The receiving dog can often be hostile, just in case the dog's coming to pick a fight! With a bit of training, my new puppy could help other dogs overcome a fear of black dogs.

There were only two pups left. One was a clown, tearing around the lounge, keen to get my attention. The other sat calmly by the settee, quietly keeping out of the way. She was a thinker. She was perfect. I named her Fern and she grew into her name, graceful and strong.

Should we allow dogs to think for themselves? To practice initiative? I wanted Fern to *choose* whether to approach a dog and her reaction would tell me a lot about the personality of that dog, and how it was feeling. But she took initiative too far with human ladies, and by 18 months of age I had to interrupt a most unwanted habit.

Fern thoroughly enjoyed approaching ladies, and only ladies, from behind and lift them with her nose off their feet. With any luck, the lady would squeal, just like Fern's favourite squeaky toy. She loved it! I could see her sizing women up in the park to assess who is more likely to squeal. Very often it was whilst I was chatting to someone that Fern would quietly sidle up behind a lady and give them a swift lift with her muzzle. They would give out an "ooh" and she would skip off, clearly laughing her socks off. Only women could replicate that favourite squeaky toy.

In her second year things weren't so much fun; she started to row with dogs. She seemed to be scared of little dogs, as they snapped at her for apparently no reason. One day, a really submissive Daschund approached her with a lowered head, yet she launched herself at this dog, roaring, teeth on sticks. There was no injury but, understandably, the woman with the dog was furious. I was horrified. Fern had had textbook upbringing. I had used all my skills and knowledge to nurture the perfect dog, yet it seemed I had failed. I spent days sobbing, so embarrassed. Why hadn't I seen this coming? Everyone in the neighbourhood, the vets, the dog trainers, all those clients, they all knew of me and Fern and now they would consider me a useless Dog Behaviourist. I was sure they would be thinking, 'crikey, if she can't control her own dog, what use is she to me?' I needed help.

I had worked with and attended the workshops of Angela Stockdale, a brilliant lady in the true sense of the word. She specialises in canine aggression. She told me even good behaviourists can't see the cause of their own dog's unwanted behaviour – we're simply too close to see the picture clearly and accurately. Angela would take a look at Fern. In a group of canine 'allsorts', Fern wandered harmlessly. She silently approached the little ones with what appeared to be grace and good manners. Yet one Jack Russell bared its teeth – what was going on there? Angela pointed out that Fern approached them with a raised tail and would stand over them longer than is necessary, rather than beside them; she was intimidating them, as if to say "do you know who I am? I'm the queen of this walk!" I'll never forget Angela's words, "Chris, she's a cow!" She was right! I could have picked that up in someone else's dog, but perhaps couldn't even entertain that my dog could be so deceitful. Some dogs do enjoy starting a row, and I had one! For five months, on cold, rainy winter days, I spent hours in fields, socialising her with a variety of dogs, interrupting nasty stuff and praising the better choices.

Fern came out the other side as a confident and assertive dog that was allowed to react to rudeness, but not to instigate it. By the time she was four, she was the perfect stooge dog and in cases of dog-to-dog aggression she was magnificent. I was so proud of the friend at my side. We clearly adored each other's company too. I would catch a sideways glance and just knew she was saying "We're doing a good job here aren't we?"

Recording her interactions with dogs on a camcorder and watching it slowly, repeatedly, taught me more about my girl. She was no longer enjoying a bit of hostility and seemed to really care about the other dogs' feelings. The footage was fascinating. I remember one day having a 'light-bulb' moment and it made me stand up out of my chair – why don't I put this footage onto a DVD and sell it? There was nothing like this recording available to the public. Other dog lovers need to enjoy this, I thought, as there is no visual explanation of dog body language out there. Understanding body language and being able to interpret it correctly is essential, as you can't stop your dog doing something until you know what emotion is driving the behaviour.

Like the Border Collie who was apparently terrified in the car. He was keen to get in but once it started he would pant, spin, whine and whip himself into a lather of anxiety. Yet when I went out to see it in action, the root of the tail was high and relaxed, he had relaxed waggy hips and his face shone with joy. He wasn't anxious, he was an adrenaline junky.

And so I made the DVD 'What dogs REALLY say", narrating the postural conversations going on. It was a hit! It was soon being sold online and in my local shop. Even the tutors on the new dog behaviour degree course, at Bishop Burton College, chose it as 'recommended reading'. I was so pleased that so many dog lovers and other professionals in the dog behaviour world, found this amateur footage, cobbled together in my spare room at home could be so valuable. Life was good.

Fern and the Jack Russell

There were times when the two of us would return home after a full day of working together and I would positively glow with pride for Fern.

Never so much as after one day when she accompanied me on a walk with a Jack Russell who was terrified of dogs, mainly because he had had no experience of dogs in all of his two years. The owners, Dean and Emma, were terrified that the Jack Russell would bite if he made contact with any dog, and I needed to assess whether this risk was real and he needed a muzzle, before mixing with dogs.

I must be honest, following a walk without Fern the previous week I was a little confused about the emotions this dog was displaying. I had followed this lovely young couple to a local park in Swindon and noticed they walked particularly fast and charged past dogs in their gardens, across busy streets, and into the large wide expanse of turf where there were plenty of dogs playing ball with their owners in the far distance. The Jack Russell barked and squealed the whole way. One minute the tail was up, then down, the shoulders were stiff, he would lower his head one second and raise it the next, jumping regularly at the owners, who were in the habit of telling him to 'get down', 'heel' and 'shut up' – barking orders at him as we went. It was chaos.

I knew that things had to be a little calmer and so I asked them to slow their pace right down, relax their own body language, particularly their legs, and give absolutely no response to any unwanted behaviour. I just wanted the adrenaline level to fall so I could see a clear picture and we made a date with Fern for the following week.

I met them over the park and walked, with Fern off lead and the Jack Russell on lead, in the same direction as the owners and the Jack Russell, 30 feet apart. We walked off slowly, but Fern, for some reason, was hanging back. I encouraged her, but no, she was clearly telling me that this wasn't right. I decided to follow her lead and asked Emma and Dean to just stand still 30 feet away from us. Within just a few seconds Fern had lay down and turned her back on the Jack Russell. Thank heavens it was a dry spring day, as I felt instinctively that we should follow Fern's example and so asked the couple to just sit down on the grass with their dog and relax, while I did the same with Fern. It was only then that the Jack Russell stopped barking.

Fern was telling me that that Jack Russell couldn't cope with any movement from dogs. I watched Fern as she turned away from the Jack Russell and pretended to be busy sniffing grass. It was only then that the owners could see the Jack Russell visibly relaxing, and walking calmly and quietly in Fern's direction. We moved a little closer, saying nothing, just lying on the grass watching the beautiful day. At no point did Fern choose to approach the Jack Russell, just laid on the grass sniffing the breeze and he, for the first time in his life, was relaxed enough to enjoy being in a park. Fern was clearly telling us all what the Jack Russell needed and the owners were both flabbergasted and grateful. She notched up yet another member of her fan club that day.

We repeated these appointments every week until she invited him to play one day and we all respected that Fern knew when the time was right, and allowed this to happen. It was wondrous. Each month the owners introduced a new friend to their dog, using the same technique and their knowledge. It would simply not have been possible without Fern.

Haunted Happenings

Bonnie, the 9-year-old Golden Retriever lived in a haunted pub. Well, Ray and Sheena the landlord and landlady told me that was apparently the case, but they had not seen these apparitions and doubted the centuries-old tale until witnessing some pretty weird behaviour from their dog.

At any time of the day, evening or night, in any room, but particularly the lounge, she would suddenly spin round and give a low growl to something behind her. It made no difference who was there at the time; it could happen when she was alone in the room.

Now, I have a broad mind and I've had some pretty scary unexplainable experiences that could be caused by other forms of being or energy but I'm not yet convinced by ghosts, so my initial reaction was to eliminate what it wasn't and look at what's left. I believe dogs have at least one extra sense, over us, and every year we discover another ability or skill previously unknown in dogs.

But why didn't what happened to the Goldie happen in front of her, or to the right or the left. Why always the rear? Why did it happen more in the lounge? During my visit to the pub I took a history of their lifestyle, the pattern of behaviour and watched the owners' recording of this behaviour. Sure enough, the dog was just relaxing and suddenly jumped up, spun around and focused on the area behind her, looking really alarmed. We studied the recording for unusual shapes picked up by the camera. Could it just be a draught or a sound from the plumbing out of range to humans? That was a long consultation, yet I still wanted to give it more thought. I took myself off to the local country park and sat there thinking.

A dog's personality is made up of three things:

Nature – genetics, inherited stuff

Nurture – the environment they are born into, grow up with and exist in

Health – including diet

What is happening to the rear of Bonnie?

Unlike some behaviourists I don't insist on a vet check before behaviour counselling, as it's often a waste of time and money and seen by dog owners as an obstacle to getting behavioural help. However, we need to be suitably qualified and knowledgeable in medicine as well, to be able to recognise when the cause of behaviour could be something physical and a vet's opinion is needed.

Bonnie's strange behaviour wasn't connected to any particular human, room, time of day or activity. The only common thread was her. They had lived at the pub for five years, yet this only started happening a month ago. Why was it happening more in the lounge? Was it because that's where she was relaxing and only when dogs truly relax do they feel the early signs of illness? Ah, hah, that's it! It was pyometra!

Pyometra is an infection of the womb. This un-spayed female was getting twinges and irritation from her rear-end because, I believed, she might have this potentially deadly infection. I'm a great believer in bitches being spayed early in life as I've seen way too many deaths from letting them get old with their bits.

When I phoned the owners with my thoughts, they were very pleased that we were homing in on a cause and scoffed in true British form that, of course, they never thought for a moment that it was a ghost.

The following day, the vet confirmed with the help of the findings from a blood test that Bonnie did indeed have pyometra and she underwent surgery for a hysterectomy within a week.

The atmosphere at the pub was considerably more cheerful when I popped in for a drink the following month and all eerie growling in dark corners had stopped.

Don't make me go out......

One of my favourite case studies was that of an 8-month-old female daschund who had suddenly stopped wanting to leave the house.

Nothing had changed at home; the same person walked her with the same equipment. There had been no scary experience in the front garden of this mid-terraced house or in the street. There had never been a reluctance to go out before; she loved meeting her doggy friends over at the park. She was excited to have her lead on, but as soon as the front door was opened she would back away. Interesting!

Sometimes you have just got to try and get into the head of that dog, and in this case, her body. Imagine you are an 8-month-old short-legged dog walking over the doorstep; what could have changed? What happens at 8 months in the bodies of female dogs? They finish growing and it is the time when they can start to come into season. On closer questioning, the little dog's nipples had indeed become much larger.

That was why she didn't want to cross the threshold. This poor little love had scraped her nipples over the door-frame. Ouch! So we doubled the height of the door mats, positioned her best friend Dougie the Bearded Collie, across the road and put her on lead. As the front door was opened, she spotted her friend and leapt out, completely unhurt, for her dose of daily fun once again.

Poppy

Poppy was a 4-year-old Border Collie who lived with her sister Rosie and loved by a Mr and Mrs Truluck, in a thatched cottage in the Wiltshire countryside. The owners told me Poppy had a fear of noises and she would no longer go on walks.

Most fearful dogs are that way because of a lack of experience, rather than a scary experience, like puppies that aren't taken out before 12 weeks of age and bitches used for the dreadful puppy-farm trade. But for this poor Collie it was a scary experience that had set her back.

Something becomes a memory when it is either repeated or significant and poor Poppy was both isolated as a puppy and had a memory from a truly significant event!

Poppy was adopted at 8 weeks of age from an isolated farm. She was a shy character, but life was good until she was 18 months of age, when a hot air balloon crashed into their back garden.

After this incident, she would run to her owners for safety when hearing bangs, seeing uplighters in a room, sails or kites – anything that reminded her of a hot air balloon. This fear steadily got worse, until she was 3½ years of age and heard a shoot start. With the sound of the gun, she ran across a busy road back to their car. She no longer found sanctuary in her owners, nor did she feel safe with their judgement, so she returned to what she thought was her only place of safety – the car. She used only to react to noise, but now anticipated the possibility of these scary things happening outside the home and so her fear had changed to a phobia. No cajoling could get Poppy out that door.

The owners called out a so-called Behaviourist, who trotted out the old chestnut that makes me cringe every time "you need to act like the Leader of the Pack and don't put up with Poppy's nonsense". Whilst it is vital that as owners, we are in control of our dogs, we must do this with patience, kindness and understanding. This character advised force, to get the lead on Poppy and pull her out if necessary. Poor Poppy would lie on the floor and shake. The owners found this very distressing, but they didn't know anything else and had to trust this person who professed to be an expert. In frustration the male owner took things too far and smacked Poppy. These two used to be best friends and that one act of striking his adored Poppy left him sobbing. He hated this approach to dog training and one day refused to do it any longer. Thank heavens his vet knew some real behaviourists.

I popped out and quickly concluded that yes, she did have a phobia to noise. Her lack of varied auditory experience when young and some frightening experiences since then, took Poppy to the lonely, terrified place I discovered her in.

We made a plan together. There was going to be six weeks of curfew, in which the owners would regain the trust and wonderful bond they used to have. Poppy would not be asked and therefore, not expect, to leave the house for six weeks.

We 'packaged a party' – Poppy's favourite toy, food, silly words that made her giggle (in this case it was "chase your bum") were all saved for the 20 minutes of fun that would happen on the edge of her comfort zone. For example, she would find a rubber toy stuffed with sausage just outside the front door, which would be brought in for a good chew. 5 minutes of clicker training would make her feel successful and drench her brain with the beneficial chemistry that it had no doubt been lacking. We gave her a supplement to reduce anxiety further and Poppy was totally ignored when the other dog was walked, so as to lead her to think she was missing out on something outside. Her favourite football was taken out when the other dog was walked and Poppy could see the ball disappearing, but have no access to it. Poppy was allowed out in one small area of the front garden to toilet, and was not allowed any further, even if she wanted to, until she was absolutely desperate to get further. By the end of the 6 weeks curfew Poppy was dashing to the boundaries of both the front and back garden to retrieve the 'party' that would have been planted there by the owners. The fun would always finish before she'd had enough, leaving her wanting more.

It was then time to go out into that big scary world. Thank heavens the owners were patient and did not rush things. The slower the change, the more permanent the improvement will be.

Gradually, over the following months, the owners would take Poppy 100 yards down the road and back again, just as she wanted to go further. The day came when it was clear that Poppy wanted to go back to her favourite spot by the river, where they used to play football. I came with them to ensure that Poppy's behaviour and body language was truly relaxed and confident. The owners by now understood that if anything scary happened, such as a glider or helicopter appearing overhead, they would simply head home in a purposeful but relaxed pace, without making any fuss.

On this occasion, 3 months after I first visited, there was a bang during our football game. The owners instantly headed home which was 3 fields away, leaving the ball there, but after a few hundred yards we were thrilled to see that, instead of racing back home, Poppy returned to collect the football! Poppy was well again, with the correct use of rules, boundaries, patience and kindness.

The privilege of meeting some people

On a cold and windy Wednesday, I visited a lady in a Berkshire farmhouse, who needed help with her middle-aged Spaniel. She wanted to get sorted the longstanding issue of separation anxiety.

True separation anxiety is actually quite rare. The physical effects of anxiety are present in the dog's body long after the cause of the anxiety has been resolved; it takes the body quite some time to return to its normal state. What is described as 'separation anxiety' is often frustration, or even sometimes glee that the owner has gone and they can tear the settee to bits!

Anyway, I digress. We found the cause and solution and I was just about to leave when she asked if we could discuss one other concern of hers. I had noticed that this lady wore a bandanna on her head and had no facial hair, but I wasn't prepared for what she said next. She was a stoical lady of approximately 35-40 years and had a happy home life with her husband and 10-year-old son. She explained that she had terminal cancer and, whilst checking that we were alone, went on to say that she had just been told that she had no more than 3 months to live. She asked my opinion about buying a puppy for her son, so that they could share in the nurturing of this little life over her remaining time and he would have something else that he could remember her by, long after she had passed away.

Although my stomach was screwed in knots by this point, we talked pragmatically. We discussed the process of choosing a puppy, training, and having the strength to live with the chaos of a puppy. Once she realised how long it takes for things to settle to an enjoyable point, she actually decided that it wasn't a good idea.

The next bit caught me out. She looked me in the eye and said, "Thank you. That must have been a very difficult conversation for you." I was stunned. Here was a lady, who had no more than 3 months left to live, leaving her beloved husband and 10-year-old son, thanking *me* for my strength. I could only wish to be as strong and generous as that lady before me. What a privilege it was to meet such a wonderful woman.

Goldie and the mouse

90% of my clients were female, for both training and behaviour counselling. You meet some lovely people, some very rich and a few that were terrifically famous, and you get to visit some amazing houses! I was invited to train two large male Golden Retrievers in a particularly grand house.

My client on this occasion was an impeccably groomed lady and together we decided that the large dining room would be ideal to train in. Training is best done indoors where there is less distraction and then when it's good indoors, you take it outdoors.

It was a huge, grand room, with a large table surrounded by at least a dozen grand chairs. The walls dripped with what looked to me like very expensive old portrait paintings.

It was perfectly quiet whilst we concentrated the dogs' attention on a simple 'sit' exercise. At this point a mouse ran across the floor. In true cartoon-style, the lady screeched and jumped on a chair. The biggest of the dogs scooped the mouse up in his fleshy jowls and stood there, quite stunned by this wriggly sensation within its mouth. It was clearly expected that me, as an 'animal person', would sort the situation. I had a lady screaming hysterically in her stiletto shoes, on an ancient chair, the other dog jumping around in glee as if he'd never had such fun in his life before and the dog with the mouse in its mouth, stock-still in the middle of this dining room, with his eyes rotating like a fruit machine from the tickling sensation on the roof of his mouth. There was only one thing for it – I had to go in!

I wrenched open his jaws, put my hand in the drooling cavern, pulled out a terrified-looking mouse and launched it out the French doors back to freedom. How I managed to control the fits of laughter threatening to burst out of me, I will never know.

The lady was almost hyperventilating, therefore calm and a cup of tea was needed before I could finish the session and go. Thank goodness for my car, it was a sanctuary from the never-ending quirkiness of the job.

Ben and the handbag

One sunny Thursday morning I visited a lovely lady with her 4-year-old boy on a tidy modern estate in Swindon. (Do you see a pattern here? It's nearly always the lady of the house that shoulders the responsibility of sorting the dog's behaviour)

She told me that their lovely 2-year-old black Labrador Ben had just started to growl and lunge at her on the way back from his walk around the block. It was only at her and only on the way back from a walk. Ben was always walked on lead and for the last 6 months had worn a particular head collar that was cheap and nasty and known for riding up into the eyes. Their 4-year-old boy comes on every walk and loves to be involved with walking Ben. They take out a bag holding Ben's ball and treats but it was now torn to shreds! 'What is going on here?' I thought. I would have to see this in action to find a cause and solution.

So the lady put the dog on lead and we step out on our walk around the block. The 4-year-old young lad pushes between the dog and mother, hanging on the lead, screaming with joy. The dreadful head collar rides up into the dog's eye. The mother holds the bag, in the hand nearest the dog, inadvertently walloping it round the head every other pace! Poor Ben could hardly see for his dreadful head collar riding up in his eye, he had his lead being tugged on by a screaming child and getting walloped by a bag that he had to grab with his teeth to make it stop. By the time he's heading home, he's totally fed up!

When I described what Ben is experiencing on walks the lady was astonished that she had not noticed what Ben was going through. She put the bag over her shoulder and changed to a comfortable head collar. She bought a second lead, which she also attached to the collar but, for the child to hold on the other side of the dog, making him feel very important and clever that he was the one walking Ben.

Peace reigned.

Puppies need peace too

A young family were frantic when their 10-week-old Boxer puppy started growling at their young children and curling its lip.

They were so pleased to have their new puppy that they wanted it to be the centre of attention and placed the uncovered puppy crate in the centre of their lounge, in which it could sleep. That way they could all talk to the puppy, give it plenty of cuddles and never let it feel alone.

But that poor puppy needed time alone. I went round there and found a puppy that had no peace. The only way it could say "please leave me alone" was to curl its lip; it hadn't even got to the growling stage, poor love.

I put a question to the children; if they were in bed and their mum and dad kept waking them up to tell them how much they loved them, stroking them at all hours of the night, how would they feel? They giggled. They were of the age that they would laugh the first night but after a week they might be tired and tell them to 'get off'.

The parents laughed out loud, "I can't believe that we've just paid out money to have you around, to explain something so obvious!" That was an hour, well spent, with a great family.

We covered the crate, so it was dark and cosy, and popped it in the corner of a quiet room. Everybody left the puppy alone when she took herself off there, yet when she came out of her crate and approached the children; everyone had a pop at cuddling.

Swap! Dog for a second-hand TV

Equally pleasurable to meeting the great variety of dogs over the last 20 years, has been meeting their people. When you meet a loving family that share the burden and desire for finding a solution to their dog's unwanted behaviour, it is heart-warming and gives a behaviourist buckets of enthusiasm to keep going.

I went to a large, comfortable home in Chippenham one evening to meet The Henderson family, comprising of mum, dad and two brothers aged 17 and 20. The younger son had met a young lad who was offering to give his large cross-breed away for a TV. The younger brother was so appalled that this dog's value equalled that of a second-hand TV, that he persuaded the then-owner to take a whole lot of cigarettes instead. The family were stunned when he brought the dog home; he had not discussed it with them and he knew nothing about the dog's character.

Within a couple of weeks the dog started to stiffen and growl when anyone passed him and his toys, as neglected dogs can sometimes do when resources have been hard to come by. But one day, when hanging around outside the 'chippy' with the two brothers and their mates, the dog growled and lunged at the older brother, causing injury to his face and hand.

When I went around to assess the situation, all members of the family wanted to be there. On describing what happened that night, the injured brother went to great trouble to emphasise that he might have done something to provoke the dog and it was his fault. The younger brother was terrified that the dog might have to be passed to yet another home and was convinced that he could be the one to bring consistent love and security to the dog for the first time in its life.

After a two hour assessment I concluded that the risk of the dog repeating this behaviour was very high. I can't remember the exact details of this case, but the memory of the way that family dealt with it, I can remember vividly.

The father gently voiced his understandable concern and made it very clear that he wanted neither of his boys to be injured any more by this new member of the family. They talked candidly to each other; openly and with such maturity that I found myself thinking 'why can't every family have these skills, to deal with the difficulties of life?'

I presented the facts to the younger brother and asked him, "If you were in your dad's shoes, what would you do?" It was a rhetorical question and, indeed, I didn't get an answer other than "If the dog goes, I go. I will leave home." The poor boy was clearly exhausted with worry. I left them to digest what we had talked about, again emphasising the huge benefit that using a muzzle can have to the atmosphere of the house and, therefore, the benefit to the dog.

I called the house the following morning. Just Mum was about. She was devastated by the thought that her younger son would leave home in this way, frightened that he would never come back. He had fallen in love for the first time in his life and that first love, that first relationship, has such power. I remember being consumed by thoughts of the family that weekend, I couldn't concentrate on anything else, I had to come up with a compromise, a way to keep the division to a minimum.

I popped around the following week and, whereas some dog owners will be cool and a little hostile to you when you have said words that they didn't want to hear, this family welcomed me as a friend. Over coffee we proposed and agreed on a plan that everyone could settle for. The younger brother moved out temporarily to a flat in the next street, funded by his mum and dad, where he could be with his beloved dog. I gave him a printed, potted version of the Dangerous Dogs Act, which I had translated into 'real' language, but also included some encouraging and supportive words, in a 'You can do it' greetings card.

It was a very difficult journey, but the young man did eventually agree to use a new style of muzzle, made of clear, flexible plastic, which was comfortable. That way he could come home with his friend and even stay over, as long as he followed the very strict rules and boundaries that were needed for everyone to be able to relax, including that poor bewildered scrap of a dog whose value to that family became far more than a second-hand TV.

Trixie

My father's newsagent, in Cambridge, called me for advice whilst I was standing on a platform waiting for a train home from Bath. I remember this because the conversation was so intriguing that I stepped on the wrong train and ended up in Bradford-on-Avon, 15 miles from where I was intended to be.

I knew their two Rottweilers well. Trixie was, quite typically of Rottweilers, gentle and full of giggles, loving all dogs and people.

A year previously they had adopted a second female Rottweiler and they got on famously. Two weeks prior to the call, the dogs had started falling out with each other and the disagreements had escalated to the point where they were injuring each other, the aggression was frightening everybody.

This foxed me; why would two great friends suddenly fall out? We chatted about every aspect of their health and lifestyle; nothing had changed. I told her that I just couldn't understand why this had happened. I knew that they fed both dogs on good quality dog food, a name I knew well, but dropped a question into the pot as a last resort. "You haven't by any chance changed their food recently have you?" She hesitated in replying, perhaps she recognised her mistake. "Yes, we've been a bit short recently and had to cut back." They had chosen to feed the dogs on a well-known brand that is notorious for causing sudden and enormous volatility in dogs. "That's it!" I said "you've got your answer"

Now normally I would recommend that a change of diet happened gradually over a couple of weeks, but the need for change in the dogs' behaviour far outweighed the risk of causing an upset stomach and I suggested they get them back on something of better quality straight away. They managed the proximity of the dogs very well and took no risks. Within two weeks the dogs were back to being good friends and any aggression, even mild irritation, was a thing of the past. They even seemed to have missed each other.

This is one of many stories I have that illustrate how well-known, nasty foods, with awful ingredients can cause dreadful health and behavioural problems in dogs, but that's probably yet another book.

Hidden suburban danger

Kane lived with his sister and their wheelchair-bound male owner, on an isolated farm in Ireland. This 3-year-old Border Collie had literally only ever met one other person in its life - the man's sister, who would occasionally visit from Wiltshire. When the owner was taken into hospital and it was clear that he would not going to be returning to his former home, the dogs were adopted by the sister and her husband, but within 5 weeks they needed professional help for the dogs' behaviour.

In the initial call to me I heard that the male dog had bitten the husband on his return home from work and the man was, quite understandably, terrified. I wasn't going to take any chances, so insisted that the dog was muzzled with a correctly fitted basket muzzle. Fabric muzzles still allow a dog to rip your skin with their front teeth and as they restrict the ability to drink and pant, should only be fitted for a maximum of ten minutes.

On arrival at the front door the lady of the house squeezed her face through the crack of the front door (which was not a good sign) and encouraged me to come round to the side door. I sought very clear assurance that the dog was muzzled. "Yes, yes," she said, "we'll see you round the side". Through the glass door I could see two large black & white shapes focussed on me, still and totally silent. As the door was opened the male dog took one look at my face and flew for it, growling and snarling. Luckily I was holding a bag that I could fend him off with; the owner used all her strength to pull him off me and at that moment I saw he had a very poor-fitting fabric muzzle. The only thing worse, at these times, than a dog you can't trust, is an owner who is equally untrustworthy. The dog was kept indoors while I had a much shortened consultation with the lady in her garden. There was no way I was going in that house!

On closer questioning, I heard that the dog had growled and stared at the neighbours and their children. The new owner told me he had bitten her visiting son's nose. The husband came home and I saw his injuries; he had bites to his stomach, bottom and elbow, and the bite on his forearm was to the bone. That man was terrified to be in his own home, but his wife prioritised her duty to her brother, the handicapped man in Ireland.

After some direct questioning I discovered that the female Border Collie was urinating little and often and the lady of the house admitted she did have a "swollen belly". I advised urgent veterinary attention and it turned out that she was pregnant by the male Border Collie.

What I saw was severe confident offensive aggression due to the dog's isolation. Yes, we could calm his emotions by improving diet and reduce his confidence by removing testosterone, but this dog was a danger to the human carers and any visitor.

On returning to my car I saw the neighbours' car pull into their shared driveway. Their young children jumped out of the car and skipped into the house. At that moment I knew what I needed to do.

To carry out behaviour counselling correctly you do need to know the very private content of people's personal lives. I would always pride myself on gaining the trust of dog owners and reassuring them that, no matter what I heard, I would not disclose it to anyone else unless they were a danger to themselves or there was a significant risk that was not being addressed, to others. Unfortunately, I had to call the lady later that day and explain that I had a duty to pass on my knowledge of such a dangerous dog to the police.

The following day I called the Police and advised them of my findings and that to guarantee the safety of her husband, I had recommended the male dog was put to sleep.

If this was not to be carried out, the lady would have needed to ensure that she was able to have it under control in accordance with that civil act, the Dogs Act 1871 which, on this occasion, the Police were prepared to use to secure the safety of this lady's husband and immediate neighbours.

I did not break their confidentially lightly; that case still haunts me. Some dogs are simply not suitable to be pets and some people are simply not suitable to be dog owners.

A 'thank you' letter

I'll never forget the handful of situations that resulted in euthanasia and in one case, the very generous young owners.

They adored their middle-aged male cross-breed but he regularly bit visitors, despite the owners managing the dog as best they could without a muzzle (which, of course, I had strongly recommended). They were faced with a terrible dilemma as they were expecting their first baby in 2 months' time.

We spent many hours together, over a couple of months, improving the dog's behaviour and deciding on how best to minimise the risk to humans of all ages. They had made progress in the little time they had but inevitably, we had to discuss the future and the choices available to them.

A couple of weeks later I received a letter from them, saying that they were shattered to have to tell me that they chose to euthanase their friend, but thanked me for helping them to make a balanced, informed decision. I had suggested they looked at their current situation retrospectively, imagining that they were looking back on this situation 10 years ahead. They told me that looking back and asking themselves what would have been the right thing to have done, helped them prioritise.

I have the utmost respect for that courageous couple.

Basil & Sally

A young couple called me about their two Border Terriers, two-year-old Basil and eighteen-month-old Sally. Poor Sally was being bullied and frightened. For months now, Basil had been "suddenly exploding" at Sally for no reason and without warning. Of course, there's always a reason and nearly always warnings, you just need to look closer to find them.

I visited the couple in their modern 3-storey house and, having been invited to sit down, I was immediately joined on the couch by Sally whilst Basil tucked himself under the coffee table in the middle of the room. As the owners and I talked about their lifestyle and the pattern of the dogs' behaviour, Sally took possession of my lap. I noticed that she was constantly watching Basil, who avoided all contact with me.

After a while, Basil appeared to become more sociable and came over to me for a tickle. Sally immediately sat up from my lap, almost on tiptoes. As she did so Basil turned away. I could see what was happening; Sally was telling him with her body language that only she was good enough for the visitor and he wasn't welcome. I had Sally sussed, and I wanted her to know it, so I lifted her back down onto the floor; she had lost her pedestal. I then watched as Sally followed Basil around, with her head held high, whilst he avoided her gaze, licking his lips quickly and turning his head away. Sally was constantly asking, with silent body language "what are you doing?" whilst Basil was saying, with his own body language, "nothing, trying to avoid you. Just leave me alone". Instead of Basil bullying Sally, it was sassy Sally that was bullying Basil! I saw them have a meal together and go for a walk. It appeared to me that Sally was constantly on Basil's case.

Over time I concluded that Basil was clearly a laid-back, confident dog, but he was being hen-pecked. Sally nagged until Basil had had enough and then he would fly at her. It was all noise, Basil didn't hurt her; he was just telling her to shut up and leave him alone. To the untrained eye, this quiet conversation is often unrecognised. Sally always apologised after these tiffs; it was okay for a couple of days, until old habits were seen once again and the pattern repeated itself. I got the impression that the same could be said for the human couple. The female was a bit of a nag and a once warm, affectionate human relationship had become a cold existence.

As is often the case in doggy households, each human has a favourite dog, whether you like it or not. How do I tell this lady that her beloved Sally is a spoiled brat and that she needs to stop giving poor Basil a hard time? Behaviour counselling is often about counselling the humans and I gently brought up the subject of how this particular behaviour had impacted on them. I was surprised by how willing they were to share their feelings with me after such a short time together and the words tumbled out from both of them. They confessed to me that their marriage was close to crumbling when they called me. Their dogs were their worlds and the division of the dogs' relationship had resulted in a division of their own. I gave them an honest, candid interpretation of the postural conversation I had seen. They were shocked.....and then they burst into laughter. They looked like they hadn't laughed together so much in ages.

I was able to reassure that, in my experience and from my own statistics, aggression between male and female dogs rarely results in injury (it's a higher risk when they're the same sex, particularly bitches). I told them that the louder a dog's threat, the less likely they are to injure

Both dogs needed more exercise, Sally was bored and I think this bullying was a kind of entertainment for her. In time, Sally was taught manners and restraint. My job was to give the people the confidence to ignore the scary looking spats and not verbally respond or rush in as that would be seen as joining in. Basil was allowed to express himself and never be told off for responding to Sally's rude behaviour. Most important of all, the couple learnt how to recognise Sally being polite to Basil, so that could be praised and encouraged.

It went well, in fact it went brilliantly. That was one of those 'I love this job' moments.

It was about that time that my husband fell out of love with me. Just as I thought life couldn't get any better, a conversation one evening turned my world upside-down. My much-loved husband of 24 years was moving out.

Within a few weeks I accepted that my marriage was over and I had to get a separate home for me and Fern. I couldn't afford the expense of the marital home alone and to meet the regular bills I needed a regular income, something you rarely get with self-employment. I was losing my husband, my home and my job.

The ache around my heart was unforgettable, it felt like a heavy weight 24 hours, 7 days a week dragging in my chest – my heart was breaking. I couldn't sleep, work or eat – the future looked bleak and I just didn't want to go there. My friends were incredibly loyal and patient; they helped me see tiny chinks of hope. One day I looked Fern in those beautiful trusting eyes and said, "Okay, my love, it's down to just me now to put food in your bowl, but I'll do it. We'll be ok". I packed my bags and, at the age of 43 took up my mum & dad's offer to escape the reminders at home and move in with them for a while, recharge my batteries and eat nutritious food for a few weeks. I wrote to all the vets from whom I had taken referrals, to tell them that, with regret, I had to close my business.

Within days of those letters going out I received a telephone call from one of the partners at Drove Vets, a call that would flip my world upside-down yet again. He said, "Don't close your business Chris, come and open a behaviour department for us". I was stunned, doing what I adored and receiving a regular income. I was overjoyed.

So, supported by a group of steadfast, loving friends, Fern and I returned to Wiltshire, still trembling from the loss of my marriage and with an enormous mountain to climb. The sheer flood of conflicting emotions gave me just the drive

I needed to push on and 'make this work'. I met with the two senior partners and talked honestly of my skills and capability in growing a small business of 1 to something much bigger – in the 15 years I was self-employed I had never needed to advertise and so with the Drove marketing behind me, it was bound to grow. We agreed terms and expectations, one of which was that I do public talks "You can do public talking can't you?" one of them asked...I trawled my memory for the talking in public I'd done and realised I'd talked to no more than a group of 10, but my enthusiasm got the better of me and out of my mouth shot "of course". That bravado was to put me through one of my scariest experiences, sooner than I had expected.

Just before I started at Drove Vets, when I was known simply as 'self-employed Christine Emerson' rather than Head of Behaviour Services at Drove Vets, a vet from the past asked me for a meeting. Do you remember that lout of a vet who had invited me to 'impress' him, from my early days? Well, he wanted a member of the APDT to work with him.

He was just as arrogant. He made it quite clear that he would be the Behaviourist, diagnosing the cause and solution of any unwanted behaviour but he wanted someone to carry out any hands-on training that was needed. I politely asked him to clarify that he wanted me to carry out what he thought was best and I was to have no say in it? Yes. Would he also look at what the dog was being fed before making any other changes, for example? "No – the food a dog eats is pretty irrelevant in the study of behaviour". I thought 'stick to being a vet'! I took huge pleasure in politely declining his offer. He was incredulous! He expected me to be so grateful and flattered. I clarified that I was also a highly qualified Behaviourist, but chose to be in the APDT (rather than the usual organisation that Behaviourists join) along with many great behaviourists, and preferred to make my own diagnoses.

I would have loved to have seen his face when he learnt I was creating my own team at Drove.

The staff at Drove Vets was aware that I knew my stuff, from helping their clients over the previous 15 years, but could I recruit, train and retain a team of behaviourists and trainers? Could I work with the vets and nurses in order to offer help with both physical and mental health? It was a dream job and from that first day, I loved it.

Everyone seemed to be really excited about the company branching into animal behaviour. Within days I was approached by a handful of people wanting to be part of the department. I was encouraged to do whatever I wanted, as long as I made it pay. The partners loved my ideas and asked the marketing co-ordinator, Jane, to set to work on promoting my behaviour services.

Jane caught me one day in the office to say that she was making plans for a public talk at a local hotel so the people of the areas covered by their nine branches could meet me. It was to be advertised in the local press and splashed around the counties. "Great" I said "How many do you think will be there?" "We'll cap it at 300" was the reply. I nodded sagely, returning to my desk to sit down, before I collapsed in terror; my head was spinning. 300?! I'm going to need help.

Over a glass of wine that night with a friend I wracked my brain about how I could do this. Surely there's a skill to this public talking lark? I'd have no problem coming up with interesting things to talk about and involving the audience, but how do I overcome the inevitable terror of it? My wonderful friend knew just the person – a talented lady near Marlborough who was a voice coach and public speaking tutor. I booked her straight away and without telling anyone at work, spent a lot of money and many hours in her lounge learning how to project my voice, stop people falling asleep and to appear totally relaxed.

In the following weeks I saw my face plastered around town and when I turned on the local radio someone was talking about me, people were excited. I busied myself by rehearsing over and over again. The big day came. I had been taking Rescue Remedy for a week and enjoyed a full body massage the day before, anything to quell the nerves. On the big day, whilst a team of us had a run-through at the venue with the microphone and projector, Jane came rushing over. "Chris, great news, it's a sell-out, 300 are coming!" "Jane" I confessed, "I'm terrified", but she had faith.

I had gone from being rejected and feeling worthless personally, to being appreciated and almost revered professionally, in six months. What a rollercoaster life is.

The people came; my colleagues at the veterinary hospital, staff from local rescue centres, other vets, dog trainers, veterinary drug company reps and of course, streams of dog lovers. My boss, the senior partner, welcomed everyone and then introduced me, bigging me up so much I thought I was going to vomit from nerves. As the audience applauded, cueing my start, I remember thinking "oh well, I'm not going to make it to the toilet to be sick, I might as well walk forward and be sick". But I paced my words to control the tremble, just as I'd learnt, and as soon as I distracted their eyes from me to my DVD footage I found myself relaxing. The more I engaged the crowd the more they thawed. I knew I would be offering a completely new approach to the usual 'pack leader' 'dominance' explanations but I welcomed their questioning and had plenty of logical proof of my new approach. We laughed a lot; it was an open and honest evening that was over too soon. Who'd have dreamed I'd receive a standing ovation? My bosses looked stunned by the response of the audience; they told me they were thoroughly impressed. I did it!

Fern and I had our own home by that time and it was wonderful to return to it together, triumphant. I eventually did so much public talking that I came to really enjoy doing it.

Within a year I launched Drove Puppy School. It was an opportunity to get it right at the most influential time of a dog's life. Yes, there were plenty of other dog training classes about if you wanted to pay £3 and get an overcrowded, uncontrolled shouting match but we were going to have small groups and be better. We were going to charge £10 per class – but we were going to be worth it!

Plenty of the Receptionists wanted to help with the new project and I was so impressed with the skill, natural ability and gentle approach of the team I chose. One of them, Sylvia, who eventually became our Head of Training, was a lovely, relaxed, unassuming lady – the antithesis of my full-on bubbly character and the balance worked brilliantly. Over the years the actual owners of the dogs at class were invited to be Assistant Trainers, as there is nothing like living with the chaos of a puppy to help you engage with and support new owners.

Karen was a client that well deserved the role of Trainer in the school. She had appeared with Filber, a gorgeous yellow Lab with a penchant for jumping up...well, anything really as long as it got him attention. He was like a kangaroo on speed. Karen was calm and patient, a natural at providing clear training. She knew she had a party animal so just used bags of fun as a reward when he got it right.

Donna was a shy but immensely talented Behaviourist, nothing got past her observant eye. Unless you are a born show-off who loves the limelight (in which case running a dog training class is not for you – the owners are the stars) it takes ages to get the courage to stand up in front of a class and talk without your voice shaking, Donna preferred helping on a one-to-one basis. But the class needed her knowledge so we all pushed her, saying it's just like amateur dramatics, pretend you're on a stage putting on a show. With repetition it became easier and the people loved her. She loved the surprise of meeting new pups to the class – you never knew what you were going to get.

We had some great times. I remember Thor the German Shepherd puppy who would shake every time tiny Jose the Chihuahua came strutting into class. This confident puppy's body language said "I'm here everyone....you lucky people!"

My professional pride was heavily bruised when I simply couldn't get Suzie the Shih-Tzu back on lead after a game of coming back when called. I had to literally rugby-tackle her, causing the class to roar with laughter at the sight of Suzy whizzing past me and slipping out of my grasp over and over again.

Bruno the 12 week old chocolate Labrador was off-lead with three puppy pals when, suddenly, nature called. As he squatted, the most enormous poo oozed out of him. The other three stopped playing and stared, everyone in the room froze in awe, stunned by the size of the poo that this pup was producing. It ended with a peak; Bruno stepped away, staring with everyone else at this triumph of art. That pregnant pause was a comedy moment I will never forget and it ended with one man slowing clapping in respect and everyone else joining in.

We had three classes of pups, one after the other. The ten minutes between classes was filled with dogs and people mingling, harnesses being tried on, cleaning up pee, a nip to the loo for us, a quick bit of advice here and there, and getting more toys and prizes ready for the next group. For every class we had to be as enthused and relaxed as the last one. After four hours from the start of preparation to clean up, we were exhausted.

After returning all the equipment upstairs to our office, we would collapse into a chair and eat cake, discussing the pups and owners. It was important we shared what each of us saw, so the following week we could give extra attention where it was needed. "What about that Australian Kelpie?" we might reflect "what a handsome self-assured fella" or " I'm concerned that Finlay the Collie was so withdrawn, he might cope better in an outdoor training class", "I could have done without cleaning up Molly's sick, did you see, she had been fed satsuma before the drive here?!" "Harvey the Lab-cross was so well-mannered in off-lead play this week – what a change from last week" or "Did you see that woman's red g-string on display when she bent over to get Fred to sit? Nobody knew where to look".

It was really hard work, but what a hoot!

Marley

Marley, the most adorable Staffordshire Bull Terrier puppy came to our class. Don't you think Staffordshire Bull Terrier puppies are the cutest things on this earth? This one, though, appeared to be a demon.

There was no settling him, he squealed and screamed through the first class. He couldn't concentrate and in the controlled off-lead play, he just wanted to jump on all the other puppies, scruff them by the neck and growl them into submission. Obviously we interrupted that behaviour and gave him lots of other chances, which had to be interrupted immediately.

The relaxed, friendly owner was hoping he would be different in class. That was what he was like at home!

We gave her a little advice after class, but there is only so much time to give little nuggets of information that might help, in a class environment and not many new owners take up the opportunity of a one-to-one session.

We weathered week two, in which we discussed diet. By week three a different dog walked into the class, followed by his beaming owner. "You have saved my life," she said. "If only you had discussed diet in week one." She had changed the dog's food gradually over the following week and couldn't believe the transformation in personality, it even showed in his coat.

Marley grew to be an ambassador for Staffordshire Bull Terriers and I am amazed that even now vets underestimate the power of diet on behaviour.

Westie – anxious to get home

The owners of one of our previous class-mates needed help when Alfie, one of our favourite Westie puppies, was 7 months of age.

They told me that he would suddenly get very anxious and panic half way through his walk. He would put his head down and pull them back home, and if he was off lead he would just take off and over any roads that were between him and home!

He was a very happy outgoing puppy at Puppy School and he still was the fun-loving sociable dog indoors and when he first started out on a walk. It happened approximately 15 minutes into the walk and in various environments, whether from the house or from the car. There had been no scary experience and it made no difference who was the dog-walker. No treats or reaction by the owner made any difference.

It's at times like this that you have to ask yourself "what happens?" What is motivating the dog to do this, and what does he get out of turning round and heading back. So I asked the owners, "What does he do when he gets back home?" They looked at each other and replied in unison "he has a pee". That's it!

Like so many pups Alfie chose not to leave their scent over the scent of more mature dogs. In the dog world, it is the dog that wants a higher status than others that marks over the scent of others and puppies naturally know that it would be bad etiquette until they have matured. That is why lost of puppies don't pee outdoors until 6-7 months old.

This dog had learned to pee in the garden and it only happens in the garden. Sexual maturity and the body's physical response to rising testosterone, had resulted in his body desperately wanting to leave his scent, but he had learnt that you pee in the garden and that was the end of it.

So the owners filled their pockets with his favourite mature cheese, stopped all access to the garden for a few days and gave him pee opportunities over the road every half hour. He had to pee at some time and when he did it was a party!

Some cases are so simple to solve if you try to think like a dog.

Frank

Jumping up on people is a common problem with dogs; well, with people really, dogs don't have a problem with it. But no dog did jumping up like Frank. He could have won a medal for it – in freestyle!

I first met Frank, a typically adorable Doberman at our puppy school. Because he had a black & tan coat he needed a longer course of puppy vaccinations and so he needed to be confined indoors longer than most pups. Apart from the odd socialising experience in the family's arms or rucksack, Puppy School was his main source of novel entertainment. He loved it!

Frank thrived, but so did his jumping up, because it worked. Despite us all telling the owners to totally ignore Frank, unless he had four feet on the ground, they still said "No, get down" or pushed him away. Of course a touch or eye contact or any verbal communication is attention and that is exactly what he was doing it for. Ignore means ignore; there is no dog, they have become invisible. Notice when they have stopped. Unless dogs are totally ignored for jumping up, by everyone, it will continue.

I had forgotten about Frank's little habit until I was called out a couple of years later to help with a completely different matter, I think it was pulling on lead. His owner met me enthusiastically at the front door, soon to be followed just as enthusiastically by a now fully-grown, adult-sized Frank.

Invited in, I entered the huge kitchen/diner and saw Frank stood in the far corner. He lifted his head like a meerkat, his bulk swaying in time to his huge swishing tail and as soon as he recognised me as 'Teacher from Puppy School' he propelled himself at me like a Russian gymnast on a mat. As he gathered speed all four paws left the ground and he body-slammed me at head height! Together, we hit the wall and fell to the ground in a heap of arms and legs, I'm sure I saw stars.

"Does he do that with every visitor?"

"Yes," the owner replied, "it's great isn't it?"

Buster

Buster was a Dandy Dinmont; an unusual shaggy-haired, short-legged breed. Like so many breeds with a relatively small gene pool, breeders can inadvertently create pups with unwanted inherited traits that show up in antisocial behaviour. Personality is, of course, 50% nature and 50% nurture, and I discovered that Buster was born with the potential to show aggression quite readily.

He had lunged and nipped at two boys in a typical family home, after being cornered and scared by them a few too many times. The parents were a bit concerned but didn't think professional help was needed. Like so many dog owners, they didn't prioritise the cost of help until one day, at the age of 3, Buster had had enough and the tables turned - Buster, himself, did the cornering. He trapped the 7-year-old boy in a corner, using a scary show of aggression; apparently growling and showing his teeth, with his tail high and a fixed stare.

I popped out to see them straight away and soon realised that the original defensive aggression had changed to offensive aggression (when the dog instigates the hostility). It took me just one consultation to discover that the risk of injury to the boys was now very high. I talked to the boys about what they can do if they are trapped by Buster and, most importantly, reassure them that sometimes it's hard for dogs and children to live together. After all, dogs will be dogs and children will be children.

Afterwards I managed to talk privately to the parents about the risk and the essential use of muzzles. They were shocked to hear of this, but they wanted to persevere. I emphasised again that their priority was the boys and stressed that it was important to have another chat, on another day, about the options open to them, should it not be possible to keep Buster in their family home. I knew what the right thing was, for Buster and that family, but they were emotionally exhausted and I did not want to overwhelm them, as it would end up with them not being able to digest any of the information.

Within days the mother called me to tell me that Buster had stalked her 12-year-old boy as he was preparing to leave for school. Whilst alone downstairs the dog had cornered the boy with a very scary display, until the boy was hysterical, screaming for his mum. The parents had not seen any provocation from the boys since Buster was a puppy, when they would taunt him a little, but along with Buster's genetic potential to show emotion very easily; this early learning had stayed with him. As the mother raced downstairs to see what was going on, the boy had turned and ran. Buster had chased the boy and lunged, biting his schoolbag. Yes, it was only his schoolbag but he had wrestled with it, tearing it to shreds, whilst all the time it was over the boy's shoulder.

The family had not been able to muzzle Buster, so he had been shut in another room and not even walked. I wish they had told me, I could have shown them how! On that fateful morning the boy had opened the door to say 'see you later' to Buster and the dog had escaped, pumped up with excess adrenaline and frustration.

I whipped around there the same day. Dad had come home from work, neither boy could bear going to school and the parents thought it appropriate that they join us around the kitchen table to have a frank conversation about what was needed. The boys were in tears. It's at times like this that good counselling skills are essential. It is one thing knowing about dog behaviour, but a Behaviourist has to have excellent communication skills so as not to cause more upset than is necessary.

My job was to tell this family that Buster was not suitable to be a pet. They did not have the knowledge and it would therefore be irresponsible, for them to find a home privately, and so I suggested to everybody that they give Buster to us, the vets. The parents knew what I meant by that, with the children present I did not need to go into any further detail. As I reassured the two boys that this was not their fault, it was nobody's fault, it just hadn't worked out and life could be very tough sometimes, my throat was getting tighter and tighter. Everybody was in tears, but I had to hold it together; it was my job.

I left the house and the father met me at my car. He thanked me for taking care of the conversation, which he said he may never have been able to have with his boys. I reassured him that he was making the right decision, that although the boys may hate him for a short while, they would ultimately understand and that this would be one of the hardest things he will ever have to do. He told me that he would be bringing Buster into the veterinary surgery for euthanasia over the next couple of days.

The next day I noticed Buster's name on the appointment screen at work, so I hung around in the office upstairs. The whole family came with Buster on that day. The Receptionist called and told me that the family wanted me to be there in the private lounge room put by for these personal occasions. We had another chat about what had brought us to this stage and I offered them lots of reassurance that they so badly needed. The father was in floods of tears and I suddenly realised that I should say "shall I take him?" They all nodded in unison, the relief that they didn't have to see the euthanasia was all over their faces, so I gently took his lead and encouraged him out of the room. As the door closed behind me, the distraught father suddenly opened it again, calling "Bye Buster, sorry mate". I clenched my jaw, my face rigid with determination to be the strong one and continued to walk calmly away, handing him over to the vets waiting in the preparation room.

Despite a calm approach and gentle handling, when the vets prepared him for the procedure Buster showed one of the most aggressive displays towards us that the vets had ever seen.

Witnessing a family's heartbreak, like that, was undoubtedly the toughest part of the job. I left the building, walked into the private garden, hid behind a hedge and rang my boyfriend. Thankfully he's a great listener. "I sobbed and sobbed and sobbed.... "It's unbearable sometimes this job, it wasn't the dog's fault, that man's tears........I hate this job, just hate it"

But of course, I took a break and carried on.

It might seem from that story that I didn't give other options a chance, like training and even medication. You'd be right in that particular case, I knew from experience that it would not be enough and while we were waiting for success, those children would be at risk. I regularly spent months rehabilitating terrifically aggressive dogs and the results were well worth the effort, but those owners are a rare bunch who are willing and, most importantly, able, to put the rest of their life on hold for many months and stick to my plan consistently. Most cannot do this, so where does the dog go? The very few highly experienced people I knew, who could and would want to manage the risk of Buster's outbursts, already had houses and marriages bursting with antisocial dogs.

I remember meeting two ladies from a large nationwide rescue centre on an aggression workshop I was running. When I posed this case to the group and asked them what the solution would be they were stumped, they could only come up with muzzles and basic training, yet they were horrified when I disclosed that I believed euthanasia to be the only option left. Whilst those pompous ladies sat on the moral high-ground others in the group agreed that we should stop feeling guilty about considering this tragic option and grow up.

It's alright for these rescue centres to frown on euthanasia and pronounce they "never put a healthy dog down" but they rarely take in a dog showing offensive aggression, especially if it's a bull-breed that they already have so many of, so of course they can say this. If they did, they would house them for life, and although some, like the Dogs Trust and Blue Cross have fantastic rehabilitation Behaviourists, there are very few people wanting to adopt a dog with such history and dogs with greater potential for rehabilitation are, understandably, their priority.

Euthanasia is a very rare conclusion to behaviour counselling as most unwanted dog behaviour can be improved considerably, if not eliminated.

One aspect of dog welfare I wanted to help change was the practice of automatic early neutering of male dogs. As soon as I felt part of the team at Drove, I proposed the practice change their protocol on neutering. We all agreed that the benefit of spaying a bitch before or after first season far outweighs any negative effect on behaviour.

However, I presented them with a wealth of compelling evidence that described dogs that had showed aggression very readily and the link between this and early neutering. The vets already had their doubts that early neutering was behaviourally safe, so when I pointed out that the neutering of shy dogs, or any dog before social maturity, could take away the only bit of confidence they have, the vets were very keen to hear what I had to say and reassess their protocol.

They didn't know, for example, there was evidence to suggest that feeding a certain well-known brand of dog food, with nasty cheap ingredients, increases the occurrence of testosterone related behaviours. Changing the diet and dividing their food into smaller meals can avoid the need for early castration.

There are health benefits to neutering a dog at about 4 years of age, but I learnt from them that it's only from this age that the risk of prostate, perianal and testicular cancer starts. A dog of 4 years of age has finished growing, its organs and bones have settled in place, and it has reached social maturity. Taking away testosterone at that age will make little difference to their personality and behaviour.   As entire dogs need to be very well trained to avoid unwanted litters being produced in the local park, we set up an adult dog training class alongside our puppy classes. These new classes were ideal to support this change of protocol. Testosterone rises at 7months of age, stays up there until about 18 months then starts to fall. So if we could help the owners through the tricky adolescent period, they've only got to stick with it until the dog is older and its personality and chemistry naturally relaxes. We felt passionately that dogs were no longer going to be automatically neutered at 7 months of age, and it proved to have huge health and behavioural benefits. I remember receiving many cards and letters from people who chose to move to Drove Vets when they heard how forward-thinking we were with the neutering policy.

Of course, nothing should be black-and-white; if a confident dog is showing unwanted testosterone-related behaviour, such as cocking its leg up against the DVD player and mounting the great-aunt when she comes to visit, they've got to have them off! Like Chudley the Corgi...........

Chudley

Chudley the corgi made an entrance like no other. Every door needed a douse of his unique aroma. Every shelf in our shop was considerably better off with a drenching of this 2 year olds wee.

On my way to a house-visit I passed through our hospital's reception, where the staff were cleaning up after him and receiving passionate apologies from his embarrassed retired new lady owner. She was desperate for help and after reassuring her that something could surely be done, Chudley was given an appointment at the Behaviour Clinic later that day.

Up until that day I had always ignored all mounting, as it was usually to get attention rather than a sexual act. Yes, this virile medallion-dog may have a good dose of testosterone addling his brain, but when he latched on to my leg I felt strongly that he had learnt it got him attention from people.

He humped away at my leg as his owner told me more about Chudley. She was clearly horrified by the lather he was getting himself into but I asked her to totally ignore him and that he would wear himself out and realise it doesn't work after a while. How smug can a girl get?

The grunting and writhing continued, I was beginning to wonder when it would stop, when I felt a wet patch through the leg of my jeans. Oh no, I don't believe it, he's not? The dog and his salacious lip-smacking slowly detached from me, spent. I looked at the lady, "I think we need to make him an appointment with a vet". At that moment the penny of realisation dropped and her hands covered her mouth in horror. Her dog had just ejaculated down the leg of Drove's Behaviourist.

I went home to change and gave those jeans a boil wash. But, despite trying every kind of stain remover and cleaner, every time I wore them, dogs would stop what they were doing and race straight over to sniff that left leg of mine. One time I had three dogs in a household battling to get a whiff of that left leg. It was a difficult one to explain. I loved those jeans, but the bin was the only place for them.

Do little dogs need training?

The most life-threatening display of aggression I have ever been involved in was from a West-Highland White Terrier (a Westie). You don't hear about the attacks from little dogs, as they don't make it to the papers.

A young mother, her boyfriend and their 6-month-old baby moved in with the woman's parents. Now, you're probably thinking 'How much harm can a Westie do?' Well, terriers can latch on when biting and tear; little dogs are often not trained as a big dog might be and like this dog, little dogs often have no house rules, which would teach them emotional self-control.

This 5-year-old was adopted as a tiny puppy and treated like a baby. It was a healthy dog, had a season 6 months prior to my visit and was being fed one of those very popular, very poor quality dog foods that can make dogs so emotional. When the second generation moved in, the dog was interested in the baby at first but then it went off it and "didn't want to know".

Three months prior to my visit the dog had snapped at the baby as it was being placed on the floor near the dog and there was apparently "no warning". A month later the dog was sat next to the baby's mother, who was holding the baby on the settee; it snapped and nipped the baby's cheek. Yet still this family sought no help to stop this aggression escalating.

A whole month prior to their call to me they came upon a scene which should have horrified them. The baby had been left alone on a garden seat, the dog had jumped silently up beside her and when the grandmother returned to the garden she found the dog "munching on the baby's head". I could feel the blood drain out of my face as I listened to the horror story. They must have seen that my face was like stone as they sought my reassurance that I wouldn't tell anyone; I simply said "Please go on", and they did.

I sat with the grandparents whilst they cuddled the seemingly happy and healthy baby whilst confessing the events of a summer's afternoon in Marlborough. I said that I presumed they took the baby to hospital? "No," was their reply, "we wiped her down, she was just bruised".

It is important to stay calm in this situation and allow the owners of this dog to tell me everything. I ended the conversation with a recommendation to use a muzzle, change the food immediately to something better and to bear in mind that the risk to this baby is currently higher than ever. That dog was due to come into season and with high oestrogen levels can also come irritability. She needed to be spayed in 3 months' time and until then, separation and if not, strict management, was imperative.

They were having none of it! Rehoming was out of the question; the owners would not even consider giving up their dog, even to someone they knew, temporarily. They were prioritising their dog over their grandchild. I couldn't believe my ears and immediately went back to the veterinary hospital and spoke to one of the veterinary partners of the practice. If the owners were not going to make these necessary changes immediately we would have to call Social Services.

The following morning I called the house to ask if they had given some thought to what I had said. They were extremely hostile to me, flabbergasted that I could suggest an operation and the use of a muzzle for their precious "baby". I would never take action behind a dog-owner's back and so quietly explained that I would, therefore, have to inform Social Services.

Some cases leave you feeling sick.

Henry

Some characters stay with you for life, for the sheer joy they bring. Miss Henry met Henry at a rescue centre and it was love at first sight. He was a cross between a black Labrador and a Bassett Hound and had the biggest character of any dog I have met.

Life was one big giggle to Henry and he loved nothing more than running, like a bullet-out-of-a-gun, from his village, over fields, to chase cars on the M4. It was a hazardous hobby.

Dogs only see things that move. If you stand 50 feet away from your dog, upwind, he will not see you. Their eyes are made up in a different way to ours; when things move we see a blur, but when things move for a dog the picture clarifies and they see more detail. Henry just wanted those cars!

Miss Henry, a middle-aged lady, was also up for a laugh, but the consequence of her new love's behaviour was giving her nightmares. Thankfully Henry had not achieved his goal yet and his owner was willing to train weekly for months, come wind or rain, to make sure he didn't. With training, he stopped aiming for the motorway within just a couple of weeks but they both wanted to join a sociable fun class to improve the bond further.

Now you must never let some dogs know they are adored. Miss Henry adored Henry but he often took her for granted so she had to act like she couldn't care less which way he went on a walk; she was going on *her* walk and he was invited on it – take it or leave it. It was like amateur dramatics and a battle of wills. Whenever we interrupted Henry's stubborn behaviour; he tried to turn it into a game and make us laugh.

I remember once at our training classes Henry wanted to go and socialise with everyone. Everyone adored the dog.

You can imagine how it frustrated Miss Henry – here's she paying good money for him to focus on her and he, like the lothario he was, was away wooing humans and dogs alike. She needed him to practice the exercise of 'leave', off lead, and show their progress to the class but no, he preferred to wander off to meet the others. One day when he did this, in a moment of brilliance, Miss Henry muttered something under her breath and stormed off dramatically in the opposite direction, to visit all the other dogs and give them a piece of Henry's favourite chorizo – play him at his own game! He stopped in his tracks, staring at owner open-mouthed. He was outraged that she was giving her loving and his chorizo away and chased her round the garden! What a recall?! What a result?!

We learnt afterwards that what she muttered under her breath was "Sod yer". From that moment on we, Drove Dog Training School, included the 'Sod Yer' cue in the Dog Training Dictionary

SOD YER – to walk briskly and purposefully in the opposite direction – excellent for gaining a good recall from stubborn dogs who think you will be there when they choose to return

Both Henrys were the centre of everything we did in our department – we loved them dearly.

I loved working with the vets and nurses, listening to the events of their day.

A Shi-Tzu had had constipation for a few days - it was causing the owner a little worry and the dog to be quite uncomfortable. The usual remedies hadn't worked and the poor dog was now off its food, probably from 'backup'. It was important to see if there was a blockage and so the radiographer got involved. The x-ray showed that the dog had swallowed the best blocker – a cork! Yes, there was a wine bottle cork stuck in its anus, so large and dry that that dog wasn't going to pop his cork for anyone. However, under anaesthetic the vets managed to remove the cork and offer it later to the owner as a souvenir.

On a similar note, prior to a routine castration, the vet was asked by the owners of a Pointer if they could have his testicles returned to them in a jar. They were publicans and raising money for a local charity. They had come up with the novel idea of placing the jar on the bar and inviting patrons to guess the weight of the testicles, with the chance of winning a meal for two. I'm not sure if they are allowed to release body parts nowadays, but that did cause a giggle in the operating theatre.

What wasn't so funny was a Jack Russell that had licked a paper shredder in the home office. His shredded tongue was repaired by the calmest female vet, with renowned sewing skills, and he recovered extremely well (although probably with a bit of a lisp for a while).

The young Great Dane that couldn't put on weight, despite every effort and ingenious idea. Routine bloods were entirely normal. Finally there was no alternative but to take an x-ray to look for a structural cause for the malabsorption. Structures were found alright, an egg cup, a tea-towel, a mug that the 4-year-old had made at play school and several toys, all swallowed whole! There were eight items in all extracted from the digestive tract. I doubt the vets had seen a dog recover so well after surgery – a weight had been lifted!

Sasha

One day, Steve the vet asked me to see Sasha, a 6-year-old Husky, who had been brought to visit us along with her 5-day-old puppy. It was the only pup to be born, but mum was healthy and attentive. The owners were concerned though, about Sasha's trembling, since the pup was born.

Sasha lived with another bitch, Rosey, to whom she was very close, but had not had much contact with since the birth of her puppy. It was her third litter and she had never acted this way before.

Sasha was shaking constantly, with dilated pupils and was constantly panting. The vet gave her a once-over and could find nothing obviously wrong. He took a blood sample to test for high calcium levels, but was not convinced that it was a medical problem and so wanted me to take a look. I popped down and had a good chat with the owners.

She seemed to be more withdrawn than usual, didn't want to go for a walk and was off her food. I asked them where, in the house, she chooses to rest at the moment and the answer was the clue to the solution. Since her pup had been born Sasha had been taking herself off to the bathroom upstairs, to dig behind the toilet. Digging indoors is often a sign of anxiety. Perhaps she was just too old to have yet another litter and by producing just the one pup, nature could be indicating that she shouldn't really be a mum at that age. But what was the solution?

If dogs are taking themselves off and digging, they want to be there. She was trying to create a den. So create a den in the bathroom the owners did. They had a second toilet in the house, thank goodness, but they were probably a bit smelly without a bath for a week.

They added a pheromone plug-in to reduce the anxiety not only to Sasha, but also for her pup, as that newcomer would be picking up stress from her mum's behaviour as well as via hormones in the milk. Most importantly I suggested that Sasha resumes full contact with the other dog in the house. The owners were only trying to keep the pup safe, but there was no reason to believe the pup was in any danger and Sasha couldn't cope without her friend Rosey by her side.

Everyone relaxed and within 24 hours Sasha was back to her old playful self.

I worked on a referral basis for many other vets in Wiltshire. One morning I came in to work to be told that one of the local female vets had been bitten on the face by a newly-acquired adult Border Collie and was in hospital undergoing surgery. What on earth had happened?

Lots of dogs don't like to meet human strangers. Most dogs put up with it and when a wide-eyed, stranger comes towards them with bared teeth and an outstretched hand they will often quietly avoid it, or sit down and put up with it whilst turning their head away until it is over. These subtle signs of discomfort are often un-noticed by the owner, but in this following case they were probably so subtle that even the vet didn't see this attack coming.

When dogs are re-homed, as this one was, or are in any confusing situations they often withdraw and don't express themselves so readily. It is therefore very hard to know how that dog is feeling and how to behave towards them. However, when a dog clearly does not want your attention, as is often the case in the veterinary consulting room, it is important to get the job done with the bare minimum of communication, so as not to upset the dog to the point that it makes *you* back off.

There are four ways of communicating with a dog:

Touch

Speech

Eye contact

Body posture

The rule with reluctant dogs is to avoid using more than two of the above at the same time. For example, if you have to touch, avoid eye contact and talking.

The new owner wanted to give the dog a full vet check and so the vet got the dog on the scales in the waiting room.

Unfortunately the dog had one paw which wasn't quite on the scales and that needed to be rectified as it would have affected the reading. Without thinking, the vet kindly looked at the dog, said, "Come on then, let's get that paw on the scale", leaned over and as she touched the paw (often a very sensitive part of the anatomy to dogs) he latched on to her cheek and tore 3 inches into it. What a dreadful experience that must have been for all involved, including the other clients and their pets in the waiting room.

She was rushed to hospital where she underwent surgery immediately.

The new owner of the Collie, an elderly gentleman, was horrified and instructed the vets to immediately euthanase the dog. I'm not sure that was necessarily the only option available and I was not asked for my advice by the owner or vets, but I could understand if the man was too frightened to take the dog home with him.

The practice asked me subsequently, to give a talk to all their clinical staff on how they could better handle unfamiliar dogs and reduce risk. The 'no two forms' rule is a handy rule to remember for everyone meeting dogs for the first time.

The vet returned to work only two weeks later, thank goodness. They did a marvellous repair job and her beautiful looks were recovered, although she was a little more mindful from then on.

Bullseye

This is an honest-to-goodness true story from one of the vets I worked with, who understood dog behaviour far more than the average vet.

A single elderly lady approached her with an embarrassing problem being displayed by her best friend Bullseye, a castrated 7-year-old English Bull Terrier (such a handsome breed). Every time the lady invited a friend around for coffee, they would settle in the lounge for a chat; the dog would sit in *his* chair and he would merrily masturbate with his paw. Yes, he would sit upright just like a human and rub himself until the merry end! He would do it at no other time.

It turned out that he used to be a bit attention-seeking at these times because the lady, whose company he could normally have all to himself, was distracted by the friend coming round for coffee and he didn't like it. The lady responded by ignoring this attention-seeking, so he took his frustration out in another way.

The vet gave the lady several suggestions on what else he could do at these times, such as a saved stuffed kong-type toy, a favourite cuddly teddy that he didn't have at other times and perhaps a good walk before coffee time, so he sleeps.

The lady came back to see the same vet about a minor medical matter a few weeks later. The vet asked how she was getting on with Bullseye's shenanigans.

"Oh really well" she replied "we're down to once a week!"

Tommy

Tommy was a 2½-year-old Parsons Jack Russell cross who lived in a household of mother, father and adult son. After waiting until the time was right in all their lives, they had adopted him, their first ever dog, 3 weeks previously from a local independent rescue centre.

I met them on our weekly socialising walk, where they asked for advice on his apparent fear of hands. As they reached out just to give him a gentle stroke, he would retreat, growl and stare. Within days this worsened and as the adult son simply walked past him in the lounge, he lunged, bit the chap's stomach and latched onto his forearm, resulting in hospital treatment being needed. I was stunned that this gentle lady was trying so hard not to shock me, almost apologising for needing my help, yet was also so clearly shaken by the danger she had brought into her home. I offered to come over after work that day.

Despite the lady of the house holding the dog on lead during the consultation with me, the son and father were terrified of the dog and the Jack Russell postured serious intent towards me as well.

The lady told me that she had discussed this with the manager of the rescue centre, who had learnt most of his 'skills' from a famous American so-called Behaviourist on TV. He had learnt to 'press down' any dogs showing aggression and this method had apparently worked very well. Within the 3 weeks that Tommy had been at the rescue centre the previous aggression shown had stopped, so the manager didn't think he needed to tell the new owners of the history of aggression, nor how hands had been used to suppress the dog's behaviour.

If dogs learn that hands can be unpredictable and scary they will, once they're older and more confident, make those hands go away in the only way they know how – their teeth! Now, aggression can be stopped immediately using harsh methods and it looks like the method has worked, but like a bubble of air pushed under water, the aggression will rise to the surface once again. Sometimes this takes weeks, sometimes months but it will come back when its least expected. The emotion that you are suppressing can come back in a physical form, with illness or anxiety, or in the same form but considerably worse.

I called the manager of the rescue centre and insisted that if he experiences any aggression from any dog, that he must be honest with future owners, but reassure them that most displays of aggression, handled correctly, is nothing to be scared of. I asked him why he believed that suppressing fear or anger, and using methods that confused dogs into withdrawal, is better than prioritising the services of a good Behaviourist. I was furious! At least he knew I was watching him and perhaps he would take his position of power more seriously in the future. That rescue centre should have been a place to learn a positive association with people and their hands, but it was too late. The aggression had been suppressed, reappeared and been successful.

After speaking to this heartbroken family, who no longer wanted this dog, I offered to return him to the rescue centre. They asked no questions about what would happen to him next. The large rescue societies simply wouldn't take dogs like Tommy and I was not going to trust the manager to choose the next owner.

I don't think I slept that night. Tommy was collected from me by the manager, who promised to euthanize the dog that same day and never to abuse dogs in this way again. If only Tommy's initial display of fear had been dealt with correctly, without confrontation, he would be alive today.

Some months later I was cleaning our waiting room floor, ready for Puppy School, when a beaming family of 3 entered the room, pulled by their lively 9 week old puppy. It was this same family, wanting to try again. We hugged; I was impressed by their determination and so glad that they would now experience the joy a dog can bring. Nothing needed to be said.

To the moon and back, with Bracken

I first met Bracken at our puppy school. Like so many other Border Collies I met, she had come from an isolated farm, of working parents, and could not keep still. She was an angry puppy, angry with the world; any request of her resulted in a rage. In a group of eight puppies only so much individual attention could be given. After a few months the owners took up my offer of personal training, but they had left it as a last resort before giving her up to a rescue centre. They just couldn't cope.

Jane and Pete were a straight-talking couple with big hearts. They had waited years for the right time to have a dog but their dream was crushed by this 'crazy collie'. We took the edge off her frustration and anger with better quality food and small expectations of her, i.e. just a sit for two seconds. I created lots of opportunity for Bracken to use her brain, to hunt for her meals and toys and learn a new task every week but what she needed, what a lot of people don't realise intelligent dogs need, was to learn to switch off and relax. Bracken needed to learn self-control and patience and she hated it!

She would launch at anything when she was in a bad mood, which was most of the time. After a long walk, she would return home and launch herself at the settee, or someone's leg; she caused no injury (except to the settee), but when she took a running jump from one end of the long kitchen to the other at her owner's nose, just to get a reaction, it hurt! If off-lead on a walk any dog, cat, car, lamp-post or tree was fair game.

But when was she quiet and relaxed? Could we learn something from the pattern of what little quiet behaviour there was?

Back in the old days, when we didn't know any better (and unfortunately from celebrity 'Behaviourists' still today) Bracken's rage would be dealt with by shouting, smacking, pressing-down and the old chestnut of 'dominating' her. That, of course, would have made the behaviour stop in the short-term, but could only be suppressed for so long, then it would resurface twice as bad.

Bracken was inexplicably lucky to be adopted by such patient and dedicated people. All I gave them was hope and direction, and I suppose a bit of personal support along the way.

This truculent teenager needed to get used to restriction; safety gates and house-training leads were employed at home almost constantly. There were lots of consistently applied rules and lots of gentle quiet praise just for doing something that was acceptable, like lying still. She couldn't be off-lead outside the home and so she was kept on-lead for months, but walked further. Initially this caused her to scream and shout in frustration, she would be jumping up on walls and people, given the chance, but Jane stuck with it and after just a couple of weeks, Bracken got the idea that she had to get used to restriction – it was here to stay.

Jane and Pete made huge progress, but quite understandably the process took much longer than they had expected and they wanted to have a dog that they could start to enjoy. After a few months of slow but noticeable improvement I spoke to one of my colleagues at the vets about giving Bracken something to reduce the production of adrenaline, but chewing the idea over with the vet, I knew medication wasn't needed. Bracken just needed time and I had to persuade Jane and Pete to stick with it.

I had asked them to make a diary so they could look back and see how awful she had been at the start, compared to how she was, but they didn't. I asked them why and they replied "Honestly? When it boils down to it, we don't think we can make it. We just don't have what Bracken needs". What could I do to demonstrate to Jane and Pete how much Bracken's behaviour was improving and that she was starting to respond? I had to give them a task that would give them an end to their hard work, and so I talked to the head of our dog training school, Sylvia, who was really keen to have Bracken start school that same week. We kept a log of Bracken's successes (admittedly, we had to struggle to find any in the first few weeks) but every two weeks we compared her improving behaviour to that at the start and I reminded Jane and Pete of this regularly. It was only when the training classes started that they created their own chart to compare her improvements at home.

One day Pete, who didn't express sentiment easily, said to me at class, "We're doing okay aren't we? We're getting somewhere, I think". I could have burst with joy, but I kept my emotions in check, as it would have embarrassed him; Pete had not just recognised the progress those three had made, but used the word 'we' – I was so glad to hear that he acknowledged that *they* created the success. I gave clients the ideas but if they don't put the hard work in, nothing changes. He saw his efforts as a team thing between Bracken, Jane and himself and that would unite them as a family.

Sylvia suggested to Jane one day that she put Bracken in to win her Kennel Club Bronze award and Jane looked at her as if she was crazy. Sylvia explained that if they didn't set a goal, it will never be achieved. I've never seen a dog owner more nervous than Jane was on the day she had to ask Bracken to show off her self-control skills to a judge. She passed with flying colours! There was no stopping that household from that day on. Bracken had to be watched; she was perfectly safe with humans but still had a volatile temper with other doggy classmates. They only had to look at her the wrong way and she would shout and 'throw her handbag at them'. Thankfully those dogs understood dog communication well and could see there was no serious intent from the drama queen, and simply ignored her. The other dog owners knew Bracken well and adored her for the self-control she tried so hard to show. She loved people and grew to thoroughly enjoy a cuddle. But more than anything, everyone had the utmost respect and admiration for Jane and her determination to go out training in all weathers to see this through.

The judging of dogs ready for the silver award was fast approaching and Jane was up for more challenge. We were seeing a real bond developing between the pair. Again, Bracken passed with flying colours.

And then, within just a few more weeks, the big one - she was taking her gold award with eight of her other school friends. Our classes were all in the garden at the veterinary surgery, where there is more distraction than in a village hall, but Sylvia had trained them in this environment, in all weathers, we were so proud of them all. The standard was very high indeed; Bracken needed to walk to heel calmly, meet a stranger, walk past and avoid another person eating cake, and stay lying down off-lead for several minutes while her owner goes out of sight. There was no allowance for a dog showing irritation or impatience, the gold award is only given to really great dogs. Slowly the judge delivered the results; walking around the garden, talking to each owner and dog individually. There was pass after pass, and then unfortunately one dog was deemed 'not ready'. She moved on to Bracken and I inadvertently clenched my jaw, as I could see Jane was on the verge of tears, even Bracken was looking at the judge pleadingly. The conversation seemed to go on forever, I couldn't read anything from their expression but then from behind her clip-board, a gold rosette appeared and handed to Jane. Her face just crumpled. We all roared with celebration and applause – that was some journey!

How could we not tell the local paper? Bracken was on the front page of the Swindon Advertiser with her puffed-out chest adorned with a gold rosette, the story of this manic dog calmed at last, for all to read. Jane and Pete were so pleased that, within a year, they got a second dog who, I hear, has been taught how to be a great dog, by example, from the gorgeous Bracken.

The Behaviour Services Department at Drove Veterinary hospital grew to three behaviourists, including one for cats, and four dog trainers.

There were training classes for all ages of dog, home visits for cats and dogs, and even chickens and parrots. I said yes to it all, even the regular Sunday morning phone-in radio shows that terrified me; unlike public talking there is no time to consider a response, the DJ is gesticulating constantly for the guest to continually talk, no silent gaps allowed. We had a stand at Crufts, offered evening chats for the public and of course, as a team, visited other dog-related organisations to learn from them – we looked a close and competent bunch in our pink and navy uniforms.

What I enjoyed more than anything else, though, was the day workshops. I wanted to pass on my knowledge to as many people as possible, really spread the word on how simple it was to look logically at dog behaviour and shape it. I was immensely proud to have these opportunities but my greatest drive was to pass on everything I knew to those working with dogs, particularly vets and their nurses. These are the ones who have the most influence on dog owners and who can get it so wrong, as behaviour is not a big part of their qualifications.

We became known as a learning centre for cat and dog behaviour. People would travel from all over Britain, and we had a couple from the Continent. I even ran a course for Social Workers who were frightened of the dogs, teaching them how to 'read' body language, to know if the dog in the home they are visiting is a threat and how to keep themselves safe. This was a pleasant contrast to my usual work as we focused on the many hundreds of thousands of safe, well-mannered dogs out there providing joy and completeness. The research needed before a course was fascinating. For the 'Aggression Workshop' I studied hospital accident and emergency statistics for dog bites, but my focus was knocked-sideways by the note at the end of their list: "3 cardigan related incidents". That gets you thinking; how does a liaison with a cardigan result in a visit to A & E?

I had reached the pinnacle of my ambition – I was enlightening vets, staff of rescue centres and other trainers to the long-term benefits of taking time to understand the affect diet and poor health has on behaviour, to care how the dog might be feeling and motivating not forcing the creature to change. I was finally in a position to influence those giving advice, so that dogs like my first, Sam, need never be the victim of harsh treatment recommended by the vet or trainer again.

Many a request for work experience was received but we simply didn't have time to accommodate them all, however, one letter caught my eye. 15 year old Amy said she was particularly keen to work in the world of animal behaviour, specialising in dogs, her letter read as one I might have written and so I invited her to spend a week with me. My initial hunch was correct; this young lady had a natural talent for interpreting body language and understanding the emotional state of a dog, and I told her so. Understanding dogs is a skill that a person is born with and I took every opportunity to put Amy in situations she could do well in and she thrived. I remember thinking 'this one's for you Sam; even the next generation are learning to avoid mistakes we oldies have made and treat dogs with dignity and respect'.

I had a talented and reliable team as well as a great social life. My friends had supported me through some very dark days and seen me climb that huge mountain, both personally and professionally, but the single life was not for me. I was ready to meet someone special and, after a hilarious experience speed-dating with a couple of friends and a month's free trial on an internet dating site, I met my future husband. He was in Wiltshire for a couple of years, working, and I was aware he would eventually want to return home to

Scotland. The day he became a granddad raised some questions between us, one of which was where we would make our home together. It had been a terrifically satisfying five years at Drove Vets, fascinating, liberating, but at times quite arduous and so the option to call time on my quest seemed appealing.

I was there to help clients, but also to make money, at least to break even but it was tough. The public underestimate the cost of running a veterinary hospital, and behavioural advice. No matter how antisocial the behaviour is, getting professional help for it is a low priority for most dog owners. The battle to generate income never stopped; I was always thinking of ways to come up with something new, or expand the really successful parts of the department.

I never enjoyed managing people and even though I had a brilliant team, there was inevitable last-minute sickness and human error. As the Head Behaviourist it was my job to bridge these gaps or find a solution, when all I wanted to do was be a behaviour counsellor.

When you are successful at something, it very often leads you into management. Success and a renowned reputation also resulted in me getting referrals for the most difficult cases that others didn't want, or felt incapable of solving. One of these was a referral from the police.

Getting cosy with Butch

I visited Butch, a 3-year-old neutered Bull-Terrier cross, in a filthy house in a rough part of town.

He had bitten a mobile car serviceman who, after servicing the car out on the street, had come into the hall for payment. The current owner, a very distracted man, allowed the dog to squeeze through the lounge door with him, where the dog turned on the visitor, biting him on both hands and as the man turned to run, Butch also bit the back of both his legs. The man just belted for his van, managing to get home from where his girlfriend called the paramedics. The police already knew of the dog, following a report of it killing a cat in the neighbourhood.

There was a vague history to pass on to me; he had been adopted 18 months previously from a lady who had adopted him from travellers. The new owner knew nothing more about the dog, nor could he describe his diet and lifestyle because the man himself was engrossed in his own anxieties and found conversation difficult.

I prefer dogs to be free in the room with me when doing an assessment, as I learn a lot from their body language; it's like a conversation. But, as I've mentioned before, the dog must be muzzled and the muzzle must be securely buckled and fit well. His didn't.

I remember walking in the room with this agitated, elderly man pouring out to me all his other distractions in life. The silent dog was keen to make eye contact with me, so much so, that he joined me on the settee, posturing clear intent to use his jaws on me at the first opportunity, and all the owner could see was his waggy tail!

A waggy tail is not the sign of a happy dog. Angry dogs wag their tail, quite ferociously, and this tail was walloping against the settee, as high as a kite.

It was at that moment that I asked myself what the blooming heck I was doing there. I'd grown up a lot in the 20 years as a Behaviourist, I was a tough bird, rarely scared of any dog, but my body's natural response to this one overtook any considered response. I started to sweat and my stomach hardened with fear. This dog had clearly become very competent at making good-for-nothing humans go away.

There was not going to be a satisfying outcome to this scenario for anyone. The dog was easing one front paw onto my lap and the other into the muzzle and, at any moment, he would get his wish. Luckily I had asked the owner to attach a trailing lead and before he could get the muzzle off, I took it, walking the dog into the kitchen. The dog immediately launched himself at my legs, snarling and contorting his muscled shoulders as he screamed in rage. 'Oh, my Giddy Aunt' I mused as I closed the door swiftly 'that was close'.

I valued my looks more than that job and wanted to use my hands for a few years longer. I'd never been bitten up to that point by any dog other than Sam, but I knew then that the moment it was going to happen was getting closer.

I had to explain to this caring but incapable man that, despite his obvious good intentions, he was not able to give this dog what he needs. Choosing my words carefully I told him that although we could improve the dog's behaviour, the dog needed someone who was capable of keeping the public safe and the dog alive. He understood.

I simply returned to the office to complete my report and left it to the police.

Another house-visit was to seal the case for Scotland.........

I remember arriving at a flat in the roughest area of Swindon to help with a case of 'jumping up'. When the dog's owner, a scruffy young man, short on consonants, opened the front door a waft of faeces blasted into my face; I could see faeces up the stairs and along the hall. With trepidation I followed the owner into the lounge with hope that it would be cleaner. It was, and so I accepted the offer to sit down, only to feel the moistness of the cushion seep into my jeans as I squelched into the armchair. Again, a voice inside my head, louder now, said "what the **** are you doing here Christine?"

I finished that consultation with a heavy heart and a promise to myself that I would stop putting myself at such risk. I always kept anti-bacterial gel in my car and waterproofs, so I could change, and I made full use of those that day. Public toilets are far fewer these days, rarely open and can be dark sinister places. When you are an hour or two from home you've got just the car to clean up and change in. As a self-employed person I could pick and choose who to work with, but in this case the vets wanted me to help all clients in all areas of town. Despite that, I had already decided that I wouldn't be going to that home again, no matter what.

On the short winter days I would wear my waterproofs when out training dogs and their owners, have a hot cup of coffee, take the damp waterproofs off and drive on to the next consultation. Rain never stopped play, so that could be another training session outside on a windy hill, where I would need to put my waterproofs back on. As the day wears on, after a few appointments like this, you end up with soggy enthusiasm and damp right through to your knickers.

One evening I was suffering from having had such a day, but my last consultation of the day, at 8pm, was thankfully indoors. Yet there I was at 7.30, biding my time in a dark, steamed-up car, damp and cold, seeking comfort from a floppy sandwich that I had made that morning, with damp underwear. I could only hope that the next stranger's lounge will be dry and warm.

On dreadful days like this I reminded myself of Bracken's achievements, the change of neutering protocol, the influence I might have made on the hundreds of puppies coming through our school, the dogs with sweets stuck on their bottoms, the one baby that was now safer, Ben no longer being walloped by a handbag and the angry dog laughing with Madonna. I had made a difference.

Donna was the obvious choice as my replacement; she was far more open-minded, intelligent and friendly than any other local behaviourist I knew. There was no need to interview; her passion for dog welfare, integrity and love of people in all their forms, would continue my legacy successfully. Drove Behaviour Services and the dogs in their care would be in safe hands.

So when my partner Scott, asked me again if I fancied moving to Scotland, I looked him in the eye and said yes! By that time I had been doing the job for 20 years and I really liked the idea of wearing nail polish instead of mud and smelling of perfume instead of dog biscuits.

I toyed with the idea of continuing to be a Dog Behaviourist up in Scotland, but it takes a long time to build up a good reputation and at the age of 48 I didn't want to start that again.

So here I am starting a new life with Fern, a loving husband and a Working Cocker Spaniel called Summer, that has burst into our life. I am still besotted with dogs, but I'm determined not to be drawn into the old job, although there is that lovely chap called Colin in the village, with an anxious Labrador, who keeps asking me to help. If I don't help him, he's going to end up in the hands of that awful so-called Behaviourist in the town and the dog will be forced to 'comply' with orders......

Perhaps I'll do just the one consultation.

Christine Emerson was born near her father's RAF base in 1963 to a Yorkshire man and his wife from Newfoundland. She moved every two years, as is the wont of forces families, finished her education in Cambridge, and stopped for 30 years in Wiltshire. There, she married young, worked in offices for plain, corporate companies and adopted her first rescued dog. This dog was to change her direction quite considerably, and bring some excitement to her life.

She now lives in the Perthshire hills of Scotland with her new Scottish husband and their dogs. It was here that she finally felt settled and from where she wrote about her adventures as a Behaviourist.

Christine can be contacted at christineandfern@btinternet.com

Printed in Great Britain
by Amazon

83656899R00058